——————— *"a practical guide to inner healing"* ———————

HEALED FROM WITHIN

A Kingdom
Journey
to
Wholeness

TOM CORNELL

HEALED FROM WITHIN

A KINGDOM JOURNEY TO WHOLENESS, A
GUIDE TO INNER HEALING

TOM CORNELL

SOZO PUBLISHING

Paperback ISBN: 978-1-969882-10-4

Bible quotations are taken from:

The New King James Version® (NKJV). Copyright © 1982 by Thomas Nelson. Used by permission. All rights reserved.

The Holy Bible, New International Version®, NIV®. Copyright © 1973, 1978, 1984, 2011 by Biblica, Inc. Used with permission of Zondervan. All rights reserved worldwide. www.zondervan.com

The ESV® Bible (The Holy Bible, English Standard Version®), © 2001 by Crossway, a publishing ministry of Good News Publishers. Used by permission. All rights reserved."

CONTENTS

INTRODUCTION
THE CALL TO BE WHOLE

We are living in a world full of broken people pretending to be whole. From pulpits to office desks, classrooms to kitchen tables, people are functioning but fractured—wounded by what happened to them, paralyzed by what didn't, and haunted by words, moments, or memories they can't explain but can't escape.

We are a generation medicating pain that Jesus came to heal.

We've learned how to survive, to suppress, to self-manage. We've learned to look fine on the outside while bleeding within. But the invitation of the Kingdom has always been more than survival. It is wholeness.

When Jesus stood in the synagogue and declared His mission in Luke 4:18, He wasn't offering temporary relief—He was announcing radical restoration:

"The Spirit of the LORD is upon Me, Because He has anointed Me to preach the gospel to the poor; He has sent Me to heal the brokenhearted..." NKJV

This is not poetic language. It is a prophetic mandate. And it's still alive.

Jesus didn't just come to save your soul for Heaven—He came to restore your soul on Earth. He came to heal what trauma shattered, to silence the lies rooted in pain, and to reclaim every stolen piece of your identity, memory, and purpose.

This Book is an Invitation to That Journey

You don't need to live fractured. You don't have to carry the weight of wounds you didn't cause. You don't need to hide your pain behind spiritual performance, emotional avoidance, or religious pretense.

You can be healed from within—fully, deeply, and permanently—by the love, truth, and presence of Jesus Christ.

Over the years, I've had the honor of walking hundreds of people through encounters with Jesus where the deepest wounds of their lives were met with His healing presence. In those moments, I've watched decades of torment break in seconds. I've seen hard-hearted men weep like sons held by their Father. I've witnessed survivors of abuse meet Jesus in memories they feared revisiting, and find not more trauma—but truth, safety, and freedom.

That's what this book is about. It's not a textbook of clinical terms or theological theories. It's a field guide for spiritual surgery. It's a journey of the heart, designed to take you by the hand and walk you through the places you've buried, avoided, or misunderstood—and lead you into the presence of the only One who can truly heal you.

You'll read about:

- Hidden wounds and how they shape your present
- Soul fragmentation and how the Spirit restores you
- Dissociation, protectors, and parts of you that need Jesus
- Trauma from your past and pain passed down through generations
- How to confront lies with truth and remove the enemy's access
- How to forgive from the heart—even when it feels impossible
- How Jesus speaks into memories, heals the inner child, and integrates you back to wholeness
- How to walk in lasting freedom and become a healer to others

This is Not Self-Help. It's Spirit-Led Healing.

The method I use is called Presenting Jesus. It's simple—but supernatural. Instead of trying to fix people or counsel them out of pain, we invite the Holy Spirit to bring up the memory that holds the wound. Then we walk with the person into that place, asking questions to help them name what they're feeling, believing, and experiencing.

And when the moment is ready—we present Jesus. We invite Him to step into the memory. We ask Him to reveal where He is, what He's doing, what He wants to say. We let Him confront the lie, restore the truth, and walk the person through forgiveness, freedom, and healing.

It's not therapy. It's transformation. It's Jesus being who He is—the Healer of hearts.

Why Inner Healing Matters in the Kingdom

Inner healing is not optional for those who want to walk in Kingdom authority and identity. It's foundational. Unhealed wounds become the breeding ground for fear, pride, rebellion, self-hatred, addiction, and spiritual bondage. You can be saved and still enslaved. You can know Scripture but still live from trauma. You can cast out demons and still carry bitterness. Jesus made this clear:

"the ruler of this world is coming, and he has nothing in Me." (John 14:30 NKJV)

Wholeness is about making sure the enemy has nothing in you—no lie, no wound, no access point. Inner healing removes the enemy's leverage. It takes back ground the enemy stole. It silences shame, heals identity, and makes room for true intimacy with God.

When we are healed within, we carry the Kingdom with power and purity. We love deeply, forgive quickly, and minister from compassion rather than ego. We become safe people for others to heal around. And we walk in the joy of being wholehearted sons and daughters of a good Father.

A Journey That Requires Courage

This book will lead you into some vulnerable places—old

memories, deep wounds, buried beliefs. But every step will be guided by the Holy Spirit, anchored in Scripture, and saturated in grace.

You may cry. You may pause for days between chapters. You may feel resistance. That's okay. Healing is a process, not a performance.

You are not reading this by accident. God is drawing you. This is a divine setup—not just to heal you, but to transform you into a healer. The same Jesus who walked into my pain and countless others' is ready to walk into yours.

And when He does, everything changes.

Let's Begin.

Let's uncover the wounds and meet the Healer.
Let's confront the lies and hear the truth.
Let's step out of survival and into wholeness.
Let's become who we were always created to be—healed, whole, and free.

WOUNDED BUT STILL BREATHING — RECOGNIZING HIDDEN PAIN

YOU CAN BE ALIVE AND STILL FEEL DEAD INSIDE.

You can serve in ministry, lead a business, care for your family, and smile in every photo—and still carry pain so deep that you're not sure who the real "you" is anymore. You've learned how to function, to achieve, to perform. But under it all, something feels broken, disconnected, or missing.

You're wounded, but still breathing.

This chapter is about helping you recognize the wounds you may not even realize are affecting your life. Not the visible ones—the secret ones. The ones you've learned to hide so well that even you might have forgotten they were there.

But your soul hasn't forgotten. And neither has Jesus. He's coming for those places.

The Wounds We Hide

Most people think trauma is only found in the most extreme cases: abuse, war, violence, or tragedy. But trauma is anything that overwhelms your ability to cope, especially when it involves isolation, abandonment, betrayal, or fear. It's not just what happened to you—it's what happened in you as a result.

- Maybe your parents were present physically but emotionally distant.
- Maybe you were always compared to others, and slowly lost your sense of worth.
- Maybe someone crossed a line they should never have crossed.
- Maybe it wasn't one moment—but a thousand little ones—that told you you weren't enough.

And because you weren't taught what to do with that pain, you did what most of us do: you buried it, spiritualized it, or ignored it. You told yourself it wasn't a big deal. You said things like:

- "That's just how life is."
- "I'm over it."
- "Other people have it worse."
- "I've forgiven—I think."
- "It doesn't affect me anymore."

But then you get triggered by something that shouldn't bother you. You pull away when someone gets too close. You sabotage opportunities God brings into your life. You can't seem to rest, no matter how hard you try. You overwork, overcommit, overperform—or shut down completely. You keep dealing with the same patterns, no matter how much you pray. That's when you know: something inside needs healing.

When Pain Becomes Normal

One of the enemy's greatest strategies is to convince us that pain is normal and unchangeable.

He knows if you accept dysfunction as your identity, you'll never pursue healing. He knows if you minimize your wound, you'll never bring it into the light. He wants you to believe your brokenness is just your personality—or even your cross to bear.

But pain is not your identity. Trauma is not your inheritance. You were never meant to live numb, anxious, or guarded. You were meant to live whole, free, and fully alive.

Pain is not the problem. Pain is the messenger. It's not your enemy—it's your signal. It tells you there's a place in your soul that needs attention. When we stop ignoring it, we can start healing it. But first, we have to see it.

Survival Isn't Healing

We are masters of survival. Some people survive through achievement—building businesses, ministries, or careers to prove they're valuable. Others survive through control—managing every detail of their world to keep themselves from being hurt again. Some shut down emotionally. Others stay busy to avoid being alone with their thoughts.

But survival is not healing. Survival is a response to pain. Healing is a response to love.

Jesus didn't say, "I came to help you cope."
He said, "I came to heal the brokenhearted."

If you're still living in survival mode, it's time to surrender the strategies that helped you get through—but are now keeping you stuck.

Numbing the Pain Numbs the Soul

When we don't know how to heal, we learn how to numb. We scroll. We binge. We eat. We drink. We shop. We isolate. We overcommit. We escape into ministry, entertainment, or performance. We even use spiritual language to cover emotional dysfunction.

But every time we numb pain, we also numb our capacity to feel love, joy, intimacy, and connection. You can't numb pain without also numbing purpose.

You were created to feel. Emotion is not weakness—it's a signal. But if your emotions were never safe growing up, you learned to shut them down or push them aside. And now, you might find yourself unable to feel much of anything at all.

That's not how God created you. He gave you a heart so He could dwell in it. He gave you a soul so He could restore it. He gave you emotions so He could teach you to discern His presence—not just His principles.

When Managing Pain Replaces Healing

If you've been wounded long enough, you begin to organize your life around pain. You don't realize you're doing it, but your decisions, relationships, habits, and identity all begin to orbit the wound rather than the Word.

- You choose safe relationships instead of Kingdom ones.
- You avoid confrontation because past conflict wounded you.

- You work harder to prove you're not lazy like your dad.
- You refuse to be vulnerable because you were betrayed before.

This is what happens when pain becomes your reference point. It controls your future by anchoring you to your past.

And often, even in church or ministry, we're taught to manage pain rather than heal it. We get good at behavior modification, avoiding temptation, praying harder, quoting Scripture, and staying busy.

But you don't need a pain management plan.
You need a heart healing encounter.

You need the Healer to step into the memory, the emotion, and the moment where the wound first formed—and rewrite it with truth.

What Healing Starts With: Awareness and Honesty

Before God heals what happened to you, He often heals what you believe because of it. That begins with awareness.

- Where am I still hurting?
- What behaviors are rooted in pain, not faith?
- What lies did I believe because of past wounds?
- What part of me did I shut down to survive?

These aren't questions of shame. They're questions of freedom.

You can't change what you won't confront. And you can't

confront what you won't name. Healing begins with awareness —but it takes honesty to keep going.

This book will walk you through that journey—not to shame you, but to restore you. You will learn how to meet Jesus in the very places where pain entered and invite Him to be what no one else was in that moment: your truth, your safety, your love, and your freedom.

An Invitation to Begin

You're not weak because you need healing.
You're not broken beyond repair.
You're not disqualified because of your past.
You're not crazy for feeling what you feel.
You're just human. And Jesus loves healing humans.

The journey ahead may stir old memories or deep emotions. But don't fear that. Fear staying stuck.

Let this be the chapter where you admit what you've buried. Let this be the page where you say, "I'm ready to be healed. I'm ready to become whole."

The Healer is already waiting.

2

ROOTS AND FRUITS

THE SPIRITUAL AND EMOTIONAL IMPACT OF TRAUMA

You can cut fruit all day long, but if you don't deal with the root, the tree will keep producing the same thing.

So many believers are frustrated because they've dealt with surface behavior, but nothing seems to change. They've tried harder, repented more, fasted longer, and memorized more Scripture—but still find themselves stuck in cycles they thought would be broken by now. That's because you can't cast out a root. You can't rebuke a wound. And you can't discipline away what was never dealt with at the heart level.

What you see on the surface of someone's life is almost always the fruit of something buried deep in their soul.

This chapter is about learning to trace the fruit of your life —your emotions, habits, fears, relationships—back to the root of trauma, lies, or spiritual access that may still be operating beneath the surface. And when you identify the root, you give Jesus permission to uproot it and plant something new in its place.

The Fruit: What Trauma Leaves Behind

Trauma is like a spiritual and emotional earthquake. The event may be over, but the aftershocks keep showing up in everyday life. The memory might be blurry, but the effects are still sharp.

Trauma affects:

- Thoughts — intrusive fears, shame-based thinking, self-criticism
- Emotions — anger, anxiety, numbness, depression
- Beliefs — "I'm not safe," "I don't matter," "No one will protect me," "God doesn't care"
- Behaviors — addiction, withdrawal, overachievement, people-pleasing, self-harm
- Relationships — fear of intimacy, control, distrust, or dependency
- Spiritual life — difficulty hearing God, praying, trusting authority, or receiving love

Most of what we call "emotional instability" is simply unhealed trauma manifesting through a wounded lens. You're not crazy. You're carrying pain your heart was never designed to hold alone.

Trauma, especially when it happens early in life or repeatedly over time, begins to form internal agreements. We start to believe things that feel true—but aren't. Those beliefs create internal structures—ways of thinking, feeling, and responding —that shape our lives long after the original pain is gone.

And these internal structures, when left unchallenged, become strongholds.

The Root: When Wounds Become Strongholds

The Bible speaks clearly about strongholds—not just demonic powers, but mental and emotional fortresses built around lies. Paul writes in 2 Corinthians 10:4–5:

"The weapons of our warfare are not carnal but mighty in God for pulling down strongholds, casting down arguments and every high thing that exalts itself against the knowledge of God..." NKJV

Strongholds are spiritual fortresses built on emotional pain and empowered by agreement. The pain opens the door, the lie takes root, and the enemy builds a fortress around it to keep truth out.

Here's how it works:

- A wound happens — someone rejects you, abuses you, abandons you.
- A lie is believed — "I'm not worth loving," "This was my fault," "I'll never be safe."
- An inner vow is made — "I'll never trust anyone again," "I'll always protect myself."
- A stronghold forms — now your reactions, choices, and even spiritual discernment are filtered through that wound.

You're not just hurt—you're bound by the structures you built to survive.

Roots of Bitterness and Defilement

Hebrews 12:15 says,

"See to it that no one falls short of the grace of God and that no bitter root grows up to cause trouble and defile many." NIV

Bitterness is one of the most dangerous roots in the soul. It starts as justified pain—but if not surrendered, it grows into something poisonous. Bitterness distorts perception, pollutes relationships, and creates a wall between you and the flow of God's grace.

The enemy loves to plant seeds of bitterness in the soil of trauma. And when watered by anger and unforgiveness, they grow into a root system that spreads through your emotions, language, choices, and even physical health.

But here's the good news: roots can be removed. Not covered. Not hidden. Not managed. Removed.

Trauma and the Spirit Realm

The spiritual realm is legal. Demons look for access points. Trauma doesn't give demons permission—but our response to trauma often does. When we make inner vows, harbor unforgiveness, or agree with lies about God, others, or ourselves, we unknowingly give the enemy a foothold.

This is why healing is not just about feeling better—it's about closing doors. Every unhealed wound is a potential doorway. And the longer it's open, the more influence it gives to darkness.

Let's be clear: not every issue is a demon, but every demon has a legal right it's exploiting. And often, those rights are rooted in pain that hasn't been touched by the love and truth of Jesus.

You don't need to be afraid of this—you just need to be aware. Because once a wound is healed, the enemy has nothing left to use.

Addressing the Symptom vs. Uprooting the Source

Imagine walking into your kitchen and seeing water on the floor. You grab a towel, mop it up, and go about your day. A few hours later—more water. You mop again. The next morning—it's back. Eventually you realize: the leak isn't the problem. It's just the symptom of something deeper.

So many of us live that way spiritually. We keep mopping up emotional outbursts, fear, cycles of sin, or broken relationships—without ever asking, Where is this coming from?

Jesus doesn't just want to mop the floor of your life—He wants to fix the pipe.

If you're constantly reacting in fear, anger, control, or despair—there's a root. If you feel numb, distant, or stuck—there's a root. If your spiritual life feels lifeless or your relationships always fall apart—there's a root.

Ask the Holy Spirit to show you the source. And don't be surprised if He leads you back to a moment you've forgotten—or tried to.

Jesus, the Uprooter and the Replanter

The healing Jesus offers isn't surface-level. He's not a cosmetic surgeon. He's a root remover and replanter. Jeremiah 1:10 describes God's process this way:

"See, today I appoint you over nations and kingdoms to uproot and tear down, to destroy and overthrow, to build and to plant." NIV

That's what healing does. It uproots pain. Tears down lies. Destroys strongholds. And replants identity, love, and truth.

You were never meant to live with bitter roots, shame-based structures, or spiritual access points. The enemy may have planted things in your soul during moments of weakness—but Jesus has come to reclaim that ground.

He'll go back with you to the original wound. He'll expose the lie. He'll speak the truth. And He'll replant a new belief system rooted in His love and Word.

Healing Isn't Always Instant, but It Is Inevitable with Jesus

Sometimes Jesus heals in a moment. Sometimes He walks us through a process. Either way, the invitation is the same: let Him in.

The longer we avoid the root, the deeper it grows. But the moment we allow Him to touch it with His presence, it begins to lose its power.

That's why this book exists. Not to modify your behavior—but to lead you into the kind of healing that transforms you from the inside out. You don't need to keep managing your symptoms. You're invited to let Jesus heal your soul.

Let's Reflect: What Fruit Are You Seeing?

Take a moment to reflect on these questions:

- What recurring behaviors, thoughts, or patterns keep showing up in your life?
- What fears or emotions seem out of proportion to the moment?
- What beliefs about yourself or God seem rooted in pain, not truth?
- What relationships do you sabotage, avoid, or control?
- Where do you feel stuck, numb, or constantly triggered?

These are not signs of failure. They are signposts pointing to deeper roots.

And that's where we're going next.

3

IDENTITY AND BROKENNESS
HOW THE ENEMY TARGETS THE SOUL

Before the enemy attacks your calling, he targets your identity. Before he steals your destiny, he sows confusion about who you are. Because if the enemy can distort your identity, he can hijack your future.

From the beginning of time, Satan has always worked through the same method: deception. But deception alone is not enough—it must be rooted in pain to have power. Pain is the soil in which lies grow. If the enemy can use trauma to alter how you see yourself, others, or God, he can build a stronghold that shapes your entire life without you even realizing it.

In this chapter, we're going to expose how the enemy exploits brokenness to distort identity. We'll uncover the difference between living like an orphan versus living like a son or daughter. And we'll begin the work of reclaiming who you were always created to be: whole, seen, loved, and free.

The Battle for Identity Is the Battle for the Soul

When Jesus was baptized, the heavens opened and the Father said,

"This is My beloved Son, in whom I am well pleased." (Matthew 3:17) NKJV

Before Jesus ever healed a sick person, preached a sermon, or cast out a demon, He received the full affirmation of His identity. Why? Because the Father knew that identity must be received before it is expressed. Identity is the foundation from which purpose flows.

That's why the very next thing the devil said to Jesus in the wilderness was:

"If You are the Son of God..."

The enemy didn't attack Jesus' power. He attacked His identity.

The same thing happens to us. After we experience affirmation from God, we often experience accusation from the enemy. The devil doesn't need to destroy you if he can just get you to live from a false version of yourself. He doesn't need to possess you—he just needs to persuade you to believe a lie about who you are.

When pain enters your life—through rejection, abandonment, abuse, betrayal, or failure—the enemy seizes the opportunity to plant identity-shaping lies. And if those lies aren't confronted with truth, they become internal narratives that govern your behavior, relationships, and spirituality.

Pain as a Breeding Ground for Lies

Every wound creates a question.

- "Am I safe?"
- "Do I matter?"
- "Am I loved?"
- "Was it my fault?"
- "Where was God?"

And if no one answers that question with truth, the enemy will rush in with a lie. These lies don't sound demonic—they sound logical, emotional, and even justified:

- "I'll never be enough."
- "I can't trust anyone."
- "Love always leaves."
- "I have to take care of myself."
- "God doesn't show up for people like me."

And before you know it, these lies become part of your emotional DNA. You're not just reacting—you're living from a false identity. This isn't just psychology—it's spiritual warfare on the battlefield of the soul.

The Orphan Spirit vs. The Spirit of Sonship

There's a massive difference between a believer who lives like a son or daughter, and one who lives like a spiritual orphan. Orphans believe they must earn love, perform for approval, and protect themselves at all costs.

Sons and daughters rest in love, receive by grace, and trust in the Father's covering. When someone carries an orphan spirit, even if they're saved, they live like they're still enslaved.

Here's how to recognize the orphan mindset:

- Striving instead of resting
- Competing instead of collaborating
- Guarding instead of receiving
- Performing instead of being
- Fear of abandonment instead of confidence in belonging
- Suspicion of authority instead of trust and honor
- Self-promotion instead of submission
- Isolation instead of connection

This mindset often forms in childhood through unmet emotional needs, inconsistent parenting, trauma, or neglect. But it's not limited to your upbringing—it can also form through experiences in church, relationships, or leadership that taught you love was conditional and identity was based on performance.

You begin to believe, "If I do more, I'll be loved more. If I mess up, I'll be discarded." The problem is, this creates a false self—an identity you've crafted to survive, not the identity God gave you to thrive. And healing begins by letting that false self die so the true self can emerge.

How Trauma Blocks Destiny

God has a blueprint for your life—but so does the enemy.

Trauma is one of the enemy's greatest tools for altering the path of a person's destiny. When you're wounded and never healed, the pain creates barriers between you and the path God designed for you.

For example:

- Someone with a call to leadership may fear visibility because of childhood shame.
- Someone called to love others may withdraw emotionally due to betrayal.
- Someone destined to prophesy may shut down their voice after years of being silenced.
- Someone with a teaching gift may wrestle with unworthiness due to parental comparison.

Trauma introduces shame, and shame causes you to hide. And when you hide, your purpose remains dormant. But healing removes the barriers. Healing unlocks your voice. Healing releases your heart from fear and aligns you with your true assignment.

The Truth About Who You Are

Here's what you need to know about your identity in Christ:

- You are loved before you perform
- You are accepted before you're perfect
- You are seen even when you feel invisible
- You are chosen despite your flaws
- You are a son or daughter, not an orphan
- You are healed, not rejected
- You are seated in heavenly places, not crawling through condemnation
- You are called, even if your past says otherwise

You don't have to become someone else to be healed. You have to return to who you were before pain rewrote your story.

Jesus is the only one who can restore that identity. Not just by telling you who you are—but by going back to the place where the lie began, and confronting it with truth. That's what healing encounters with Jesus do: they restore identity by revealing the Father's heart.

Healing the False Identity

The good news is: you don't have to keep living from the wound. When you allow Jesus into the places where identity was distorted, He:

- Reveals the lie
- Speaks the truth
- Confronts the orphan mindset
- Reconnects you to the Father
- Releases the spirit of sonship
- Realigns your purpose

Romans 8:15 says:

"For you did not receive the spirit of slavery to fall back into fear, but you have received the Spirit of adoption as sons, by whom we cry, 'Abba! Father!'" ESV

True healing restores your ability to say "Abba" again—not just intellectually, but emotionally. You stop relating to God through fear or obligation. You begin to trust, receive, rest, and walk in confidence. That's what sons and daughters do.

Practical Steps to Begin Healing Your Identity

1. Ask the Holy Spirit to show you where you've believed lies about who you are.
2. Write down phrases or beliefs that sound like fear, shame, or rejection.

3. Ask Jesus where those beliefs began—what memory, moment, or relationship planted them?
4. Invite Him into that place and ask Him to speak truth.
5. Renounce the lie, declare the truth, and release the false identity.
6. Receive the Father's voice again—let Him call you son, daughter, beloved.
7. Surround yourself with people who reinforce the truth of your identity, not the echo of your pain.

You Are Who God Says You Are

Healing doesn't make you someone new—it restores you to the someone you've always been in the heart of God.

The world may have labeled you. Religion may have confined you. Pain may have masked you. But the voice of the Father still calls out:

"This is My beloved child, in whom I am well pleased."

Let that voice become louder than the pain. Let His truth shatter the lies. Let His love dismantle the orphan spirit. And let the healing journey continue—because your identity is too important to be left in pieces.

4

SHATTERED SOULS
UNDERSTANDING SOUL FRAGMENTS AND THEIR HEALING

"Something shattered inside me."

It's a phrase I've heard more times than I can count. Sometimes it's spoken through tears. Sometimes through numbness. Sometimes through anger or shame. But the common thread is this: something in the soul broke when the trauma hit. And while the person kept living, functioning, even ministering—something inside stopped growing, stopped trusting, or stopped showing up altogether.

This is the reality of soul fragmentation. It's not just poetic language—it's a spiritual and emotional reality that explains why some believers can't seem to move forward no matter how much truth they know. It's why people feel stuck in the same emotions, beliefs, and behaviors—even after deliverance or prayer. Because what's broken must be healed, and what's shattered must be brought back together.

What Are Soul Fragments?

The soul, biblically speaking, is the mind, will, and emotions. It's the seat of identity, desire, and memory. When trauma enters, especially in early development or in severe situations, the soul can split or fragment as a survival mechanism.

These fragments are not demonic. They are wounded parts of the self—sections of the soul that become disconnected from the core because the pain was too much to bear.

A soul fragment:

- Often holds a specific memory or emotion
- May remain "stuck" at the age or moment the trauma occurred
- May carry intense fear, grief, shame, or rage
- Sometimes creates what feels like a "different self" inside the person
- Can be triggered by present situations that mirror past wounds
- May come forward involuntarily during stress or emotional overwhelm

These parts aren't enemies. They're protectors, survivors, and carriers of pain. And they're waiting for Jesus to come into their reality—not just to explain the pain, but to heal it and bring them home.

Biblical and Spiritual Insights on Fragmentation

While the Bible may not use the clinical term "fragmentation," the concept is woven throughout Scripture:

Psalm 23:3 says:

"He restores my soul..." NKJV

The word "restore" in Hebrew (shuwb) implies returning something to its original place—bringing back what was lost or broken.

Psalm 147:3 says:

"He heals the brokenhearted and binds up their wounds." NKJV

The word for "brokenhearted" here means shattered in inner being. The idea is not just emotional sadness—it's a fractured soul. God's healing includes not only comfort but binding and reintegrating what has been torn apart.

Isaiah 61:1 declares:

"He has sent Me to bind up the brokenhearted..." NKJV

Again, the implication is the gathering of scattered pieces, like a potter reclaiming shards of clay and molding them back into something beautiful.

The Gadarene demoniac in Mark 5 also offers insight. He was living among tombs, cutting himself, and crying out—a picture of torment, fragmentation, and dissociation. After his encounter with Jesus, Scripture says he was "clothed and in his right mind." Healing didn't just mean deliverance—it meant restoration of identity and integration of self.

How Fragments Are Formed

Soul fragmentation typically occurs when the emotional and psychological pain is so great that the person cannot process it as a whole. The soul essentially compartmentalizes the experience to protect itself. These experiences may include:

- Childhood abuse or neglect
- Repeated trauma or betrayal
- Sexual violence
- Abandonment by parents or caregivers
- Sudden death or loss
- Intense fear or threat to life
- Ritual abuse or mind control
- Rejection at a core identity level

In children especially, who don't have the emotional tools to process deep pain, the soul divides rather than collapses. This division may not always be noticeable on the outside, but over time it affects emotions, memory, behavior, and even spiritual experience.

The result? A person who looks fine externally but internally lives disconnected from themselves.

Recognizing Fragmentation in Real Life

Here are a few signs that soul fragmentation may be present:

- Feeling "stuck" at a certain emotional age or moment
- Having gaps in memory or blackouts
- Sudden emotional shifts or mood swings
- Feeling like "a part of me believes," but another part resists
- Reacting in childlike or irrational ways to certain triggers

- Knowing truth cognitively but feeling disconnected from it emotionally
- Feeling like multiple parts of you are in conflict
- Extreme fear, rage, or grief that seems disproportionate or inaccessible

These aren't signs of weakness. They're signs of pain that hasn't been integrated or healed.

The Holy Spirit's Role in Restoration and Integration

Healing soul fragments is not about applying a technique—it's about partnering with the Holy Spirit, who is the ultimate Restorer of the soul.

Here's what that process looks like:

1. Invite the Holy Spirit to bring up the fragment that needs healing. This is often done in a safe, Spirit-filled prayer setting.
2. Ask the person where they are—what memory, environment, or scene is present.
3. Help them identify who's there, what's happening, and what they're feeling.
4. Listen for lies the fragment is believing—this is key.
5. Present Jesus into that memory. Ask Jesus to reveal Himself to the fragment.
6. Watch what Jesus does. Ask what He's saying, where He is standing, and how the fragment is responding.
7. Invite the person to release lies, forgive where needed, and let Jesus heal the pain.
8. Ask Jesus to integrate the fragment back into the core person. Often, the person will sense the part growing up, merging, or stepping back into unity.

9. Bless the integration. Speak wholeness, identity, and safety over the person.
10. Close with peace, thanking the Holy Spirit for His work.

This is a sacred moment. Often, people feel immediate release, wholeness, and clarity. It's not just emotional—it's spiritual deliverance through love.

Healing Is a Journey, Not a Formula

Not all fragments heal in one session. Some are layered. Some carry multiple traumas. Some are afraid to trust. But the more consistently a person encounters Jesus in these places, the more healing occurs.

This is why patience, compassion, and discernment are critical. We don't force healing. We facilitate encounter.

Remember: fragments aren't obstacles—they're parts of the person waiting for Jesus. They are often protectors, intercessors, and even carriers of powerful gifts. Once healed, these parts reintegrate into the core person, and wholeness becomes not just a hope—but a reality.

You Were Never Meant to Live in Pieces

Jesus died for every part of you—not just the visible, functional parts, but the hidden, shattered, and silent ones too.

He is not overwhelmed by your brokenness. He is drawn to it. He does not shame your fragmentation. He redeems it. Your healing is His joy.

You don't have to keep disassociating to survive. You don't have to pretend you're whole when you feel like you're living in a thousand pieces. Jesus is the Restorer of souls. He doesn't throw away shattered vessels—He gathers every fragment and makes something more glorious than before.

If you feel like part of you is missing... this chapter was for you. And the next step is letting Jesus lead you into that moment—where He was always present—and finally, finally, bring it home.

5

FRAGMENTED WITHIN

UNDERSTANDING DISSOCIATIVE DISORDERS
AND INNER HEALING

For some people, pain comes and goes. For others, it comes and fractures. And instead of fading, it fragments. It becomes a dividing line between what they feel and what they can't feel... between who they are and who they become to survive.

This is what dissociation looks like.

Most people know about trauma. Fewer understand how the mind and soul adapt to it. Dissociation is the soul's emergency exit—a God-given psychological mechanism that protects a person from being overwhelmed by terror, abuse, or powerlessness. But what begins as protection can later become a prison.

In this chapter, we'll explore what dissociation is, how it develops, what disorders may stem from it, and how inner healing and Spirit-led ministry can gently walk people toward wholeness. This is sacred ground—and those navigating it are not "crazy," weak, or too broken. They're survivors. And the Healer knows every part of them.

What Is Dissociation?

Dissociation is the psychological and emotional disconnection of a person from aspects of their self, memory, emotions, body, or environment. It's not always dramatic. It can be subtle —spacing out, forgetting chunks of time, or feeling like you're watching your life from outside yourself.

At its core, dissociation is the soul's attempt to distance itself from unbearable pain.

It's what happens when the internal overwhelm is too intense, and the only way to survive is to shut off or segment the experience.

Think of it like emotional shock. When someone is in physical trauma, the body can go into shock—numbing the pain temporarily. Dissociation is like emotional or soul-shock. It allows a person to endure what would otherwise be intolerable.

Types of Dissociative Experiences

Not all dissociation is the same. It exists on a spectrum— from mild to severe. Let's look at some categories:

1. Depersonalization

This involves feeling detached from yourself. You might feel like you're watching your life like a movie or that your body doesn't feel like your own. People describe it as being numb, robotic, or not really "in" their body.

2. Derealization

This is the sense that the world around you is unreal or dreamlike. Colors may seem faded or too bright. Sounds may be distant or distorted. Time may feel slow or fast. It's like being behind glass—present but disconnected.

3. Dissociative Amnesia

This is the inability to recall personal information, usually related to a traumatic or stressful event. These memory gaps go beyond normal forgetfulness and may involve significant chunks of time.

4. Dissociative Identity Disorder (DID)

Formerly known as Multiple Personality Disorder, DID involves the presence of two or more distinct identity states or parts, each with their own ways of perceiving, relating to, and thinking about the world and self. These parts may have names, roles, ages, or even different handwriting or voices.

DID isn't a disorder of fantasy—it's a response to chronic, repeated trauma, often beginning in early childhood. It is the brain and soul's ultimate act of survival when pain becomes unmanageable.

Why Dissociation Happens: A Protective Response

Dissociation is not weakness—it's strategy.

When a child is trapped in a situation they can't escape, and the nervous system is overwhelmed by fear, abandonment, or violation, dissociation becomes the escape hatch. If the body can't flee, the soul does.

Over time, if trauma is repeated or unaddressed, the disconnect becomes reinforced. The person may not even remember what happened—but their body and soul do. And parts of them begin to carry the pain, fear, rage, shame, or numbness that the core self can't bear.

This is where soul fragmentation (as discussed in Chapter 4) and dissociation intertwine. Some fragmented parts may develop distinct characteristics or roles—especially in DID. These aren't demons—they're traumatized parts of the person who need Jesus, safety, and integration.

Understanding the Complexity of Dissociative Identity Disorder (DID)

DID is often misunderstood—even in Christian circles. Some believe it's purely demonic. Others dismiss it as exaggerated. But real people live with this reality every day, and the church must become a place where they are seen, safe, and healed.

People with DID may:

- Lose time or have memory gaps
- Hear internal conversations or feel like someone else is "taking over"
- Have different handwriting or preferences at different times
- Carry internal conflict between parts
- Struggle with intense self-loathing, fear, or shame
- Appear high-functioning but feel broken internally

Each part (also called an alter or identity state) may serve a function:

- A child part may hold grief or fear
- A protector part may be angry, numb, or defensive
- A manager part may keep the person high-achieving or people-pleasing
- A spiritual part may seek God or reject Him based on trauma

Healing doesn't come by suppressing or "casting out" these parts. It comes through listening, loving, inviting Jesus into each part's pain, and helping them find safety enough to reintegrate.

How the Church Has Misunderstood Dissociation

Sadly, many well-meaning believers have done harm by oversimplifying dissociation.

Common errors include:

- Labeling it demonic when it's trauma-based
- Demanding instant integration without honoring the person's process
- Quoting Scripture at pain instead of presenting Jesus to the part
- Praying for deliverance when what's needed is comfort and understanding
- Ignoring the signs because it feels too complex or uncomfortable

While demonic oppression can co-exist with dissociation, they are not the same thing. The person needs both compassion and authority—truth and tenderness.

Ministering to Dissociated People

When ministering to someone with dissociation or DID, the goal is not to fix or force. The goal is to facilitate encounters with Jesus where each part feels seen, heard, and safe to heal.

Here are key steps:

1. Create a Safe Space
People won't bring forward parts unless they feel safe. Build trust. Be consistent. Don't be shocked or intimidated.

2. Invite the Holy Spirit to Guide the Session
Ask Him to bring up the part He wants to work with. It may be a child part, a protector, or one in pain.

3. Engage the Part with Honor
Talk directly to the part that comes forward. Ask them how old they are, what they believe, what they need, and if they'd be willing to meet Jesus.

4. Present Jesus into Their World
Let them describe what they see. Ask Jesus to come into that memory, moment, or space. Let them describe what He does, where He stands, what He says.

5. Let Jesus Speak the Truth
If the part believes a lie—like "I'm bad," "I'm alone," or "God hates me"—ask Jesus, "Is that true?" Let His truth break the lie.

6. Ask about Forgiveness
If the part is holding unforgiveness, help them ask Jesus

about it. Many parts are waiting for permission to let go of hatred, fear, or vows.

7. Invite Integration
If the part is ready, ask Jesus to help them come back into the core self. Some will grow up, merge, or rest. Don't rush. Some parts take time.

8. Debrief and Pray Peace
After the encounter, speak peace over the person. Affirm the progress. Encourage rest and follow-up.

Wholeness Is Possible

I've seen people with years of dissociative struggle begin to experience real healing. Integration is possible. Wholeness is God's will. Jesus is patient, present, and powerful in every room of the soul.

You are not disqualified by your fragmentation. You are not too complex for the Kingdom. You are deeply known by God.

To the one who feels lost inside themselves:
Jesus knows every part of you—and He's not afraid of any of them.

To the one who doesn't remember what happened, but knows something is wrong:
Jesus sees what you can't. He remembers what was stolen. He restores what was shattered.

To the one walking alongside someone with DID:
Be steady. Be safe. Be Spirit-filled. And never stop pointing every part to Jesus.

6

THE GUARDIANS WITHIN

UNDERSTANDING PROTECTOR PARTS AND THEIR HEALING

You weren't weak when you built walls. You were surviving. Long before you understood what trauma, fragmentation, or dissociation was, something inside you instinctively rose up to protect you. It may have come in the form of anger, coldness, over-control, perfectionism, people-pleasing, or withdrawal—but it was a part of you that said, "Never again. I won't let that happen again."

These are the protector parts.

They are not demons. They are not your enemy. They are parts of your soul that stepped in when no one else did. And while they may be causing chaos in your present, they were formed out of necessity in your past.

In this chapter, we'll explore what protector parts are, how they function, the different forms they can take, and how to gently invite them into the healing presence of Jesus. If you've ever wondered why you react so strongly, shut down so easily, or sabotage closeness when it's offered, you're about to meet the guardians within—and begin the journey of helping them lay down their swords and finally find rest.

What Are Protector Parts?

Protector parts are soul fragments that developed in response to pain, trauma, or vulnerability. Their purpose? To protect the inner self from further harm.

They often form when the core self is overwhelmed by fear, shame, or betrayal. In those moments, something rises up internally to make sure it never happens again. These protectors don't ask for permission—they just show up. They may present as:

- The Angry One — lashes out, defends, attacks
- The Numb One — shuts down, disconnects, avoids emotion
- The Compliant One — appeases, pleases, avoids conflict
- The Controlling One — micromanages, manipulates, dominates
- The Performer — overachieves, distracts, earns love
- The Watcher — observes, stays detached, avoids vulnerability
- The Hyper-Spiritual One — hides behind Scripture, avoids feelings

Each of these parts has a strategy—crafted not by logic, but by pain. And these strategies often worked for a season. But what protected you in the past can imprison you in the present.

The Role of Protectors in the System

In a dissociated or fragmented internal system, protectors often serve as gatekeepers. They keep the more wounded or vulnerable parts from coming to the surface. They manage the external world. They prevent triggers, monitor safety, and sometimes even block ministry moments—out of fear that healing might open doors to more pain.

They're not trying to rebel. They're trying to protect. But they don't know that Jesus is safe. They've never been introduced to Him.

That's why healing protectors requires honor, patience, and spiritual discernment. You cannot bully a protector into submission. You must gain their trust. And once they realize Jesus is safer than they are, most of them will gladly step back.

How Protectors Speak and Act

You may recognize a protector showing up when you or someone you're ministering to:

- Suddenly gets defensive during a prayer session
- Becomes emotionally numb or "blank" when touching on a wound
- Switches to humor, sarcasm, or spiritual clichés to avoid feelings
- Argues with truth, resists prayer, or says "this isn't working"
- Shuts down entirely or leaves the conversation
- Turns cold or aggressive when vulnerable parts are mentioned

These are not random behaviors. These are protectors

doing their job. And the job they were given—keep the system safe—has never been revisited.

Ministering to Protector Parts with Honor

The key to healing protectors is honor. You must speak to them as people, not as problems. They were formed with purpose, even if their methods are now causing damage. Here's how to engage with a protector part during inner healing:

1. Acknowledge Their Role
Start with compassion:
"I can tell you've been working hard to keep this person safe. Thank you for what you've done to help them survive."
This disarms the need to fight.

2. Ask Their Name or Function
Ask something like:
"What do I call you? What's your role? How old are you?"You might hear: "I'm the angry one," "I don't let anyone close," or "I'm the one who never sleeps."

3. Ask Why They're There
"What are you protecting them from? When did you start helping them?"
Often, protectors will describe an origin wound—abuse, betrayal, abandonment. This opens the door to healing the wound that created them.

4. Introduce Jesus
This is the most important part. Ask the protector:
"Would it be okay if Jesus came into this space with you?"

Many will say no at first. They don't trust Him yet. That's okay. Ask them why, and invite Jesus to respond. Sometimes the protector has never met Jesus for themselves. When they do, everything changes.

5. Ask if They Want to Rest

"Would you like to lay down your sword? Would you like to not have to be in charge anymore?"
Often, these parts are exhausted. They've been on guard 24/7 for years. When they feel safe, many are ready to let go.

6. Invite Jesus to Take the Burden

Ask Jesus to take the protector by the hand and walk with them. Invite Him to give them a new role, a new name, or simply bring them into integration. Some protectors will merge immediately. Others will want to observe and stay nearby.

When Protectors Are Angry or Defiant

Some protectors are hostile. They don't trust people, pastors, or even God. But their anger is rooted in deep, unresolved pain. These are the "I hate God" parts, the ones who shut down every time you pray. You must treat them like wounded children, not rebellious spirits.
Ask:

- "What happened that made you feel this way?"
- "Where was God when that happened?"
- "Would it be okay if you asked Him yourself?"

Let them hear from Jesus directly. Most angry protectors are actually protecting the wounded child from the pain of being disappointed again.

When they see that Jesus doesn't flinch, doesn't get defensive, and doesn't abandon them, even the angriest protectors often soften.

Restoration of the Inner System

When protectors are healed, the entire internal system begins to settle. The person may notice:

- Greater peace and emotional stability
- Less sabotage or internal resistance
- Improved connection with God and others
- Increased clarity and sense of identity
- A deeper ability to feel and express emotions

It's like the internal security team finally goes off duty. The person no longer has to be "on guard" all the time. They can finally rest.

This doesn't happen in one session. It's a process of building trust, listening deeply, and walking gently. But the reward is profound: a soul that no longer has to fight itself.

Helping Your Own Protectors Heal

If you're the one with protector parts, here are steps to begin:

1. Acknowledge them
Don't shame or ignore them. Say, "Thank you for trying to protect me. You did the best you could."

2. Ask Jesus to speak to them
Invite Him to reveal Himself to each one. Ask what He wants them to know.

3. Write to them
Sometimes journaling to your parts can help surface emotion and memory.

4. Let others help
Don't try to heal your protectors alone. Trusted pastors, counselors, or mentors can walk with you.

5. Don't rush
Some protectors need time. That's okay. The goal is safety, not speed.

Jesus Is the Better Protector

For every protector you've built, there is a better one waiting. His name is Jesus.

- He's the one who never sleeps or slumbers.
- He's the one who never leaves or forsakes.
- He's the one who laid down His life to cover yours.
- He's the one who sees the pain, the rage, the walls— and still stays.

You don't have to keep defending yourself. You don't have to keep running. There is One who is strong enough to guard your soul and tender enough to carry your heart.

To the protector parts reading this through the eyes of the person you guard:

You are seen. You are honored. And you are invited into healing.

Jesus has never lost a battle. And He'll never lose you.

7

ESCAPING THE DARKNESS
UNDERSTANDING RITUAL ABUSE AND GOD'S HEALING POWER

There is a type of evil that is not just personal, but planned. Not just painful, but perverse. A darkness so systematic, intentional, and hidden that its survivors often wonder if anyone will ever believe them, let alone understand.

This is the world of ritual abuse.

Behind closed doors, cloaked in secrecy and shame, there are individuals—many of them children—who have suffered horrific acts at the hands of others in the name of false power, twisted religion, or spiritual control. It's not just abuse—it's organized, repeated, and often spiritual in nature. And its effects can fracture a soul like glass.

But even this level of darkness is no match for the power of Jesus.

In this chapter, we will expose what ritual abuse is, explore its connection to dissociation, soul fragmentation, and spiritual bondage, and—most importantly—walk into the truth that no one is too broken for God's healing power.

What Is Ritual Abuse?

Ritual abuse is a form of abuse that is systematic, repetitive, and often includes occult or religious symbolism and ceremonies. It typically involves:

- Extreme physical, sexual, and emotional abuse
- Programming or mind control
- Use of spiritual language or demonic invocation
- Repetition of trauma to create internal divisions
- Fear-based control mechanisms (threats, vows, punishments)
- Hidden agendas, often passed down generationally

The goal of ritual abuse is not only to harm the body but to fracture the soul—to create internal chaos, break the will, and open spiritual doors for bondage.

This abuse is often done under the cover of religious institutions, secret societies, or cult-like groups. Victims are typically gaslit into silence, sometimes even from a young age, with threats that keep them bound in fear and confusion for years—even decades.

The Spiritual Component: Darkness Masquerading as Light

What makes ritual abuse particularly insidious is that it often masquerades as something spiritual. Victims may be told the abuse is God's will. Scriptures may be twisted to justify pain. Ceremonies may mimic baptism, communion, or other spiritual acts—creating deep spiritual confusion.

In many cases, demonic entities are invoked, and soul fragments or dissociated parts are assigned to specific roles within a person's internal system. These are sometimes referred to as "programmed alters," and they may:

- Protect secrets
- Block access to memories
- Perform rituals
- Resist prayer or Christian environments
- Manifest confusion, rage, or numbness when healing is attempted

This is spiritual warfare at its most strategic. But God's Kingdom is greater.

Connection to Dissociation and Fragmentation

As discussed in earlier chapters, when trauma is too great, the soul fragments. In ritual abuse, this fragmentation is often intentional.

The abuse is designed to:

- Break the mind through fear and repetition
- Create parts that can be programmed for specific functions
- Ensure secrecy by compartmentalizing memories
- Allow demonic access through spiritual openings or vows

Some survivors may have hundreds of parts or alters—each with a role, a name, and a purpose. Some of these may be loyal to abusers. Others may be protectors or wounded children. Still others may not know Jesus is real—or safe.

This is why healing from ritual abuse takes time, spiritual sensitivity, and deep compassion. We cannot rush the process. But with the help of the Holy Spirit, we can guide each part back to the One who never left them.

Ministering to Survivors of Ritual Abuse

Survivors of ritual abuse need more than counseling—they need Spirit-led healing. But they also need safety, honor, and patience. Here's how to begin:

1. Create a Safe Environment
Survivors need consistent, non-controlling relationships. They've lived in fear. Safety is foundational for healing.

2. Discern What's Happening Spiritually
Not everything is a demon, and not everything is a soul part. Some parts are wounded fragments. Others may be under demonic oppression. We must ask the Holy Spirit for discernment—daily.

3. Invite Jesus Into the Internal World
Just as in other inner healing work, you must engage each part. Ask them their name, role, age, and beliefs. Ask if they'd like to meet Jesus. Often, Jesus will appear in incredibly personal ways to each part, bringing peace, safety, and truth.

4. Break Vows and Programming
Ritual abuse often involves vows—spoken or unspoken agreements made in fear. These must be renounced in Jesus' name. You can say something like: *"In the name of Jesus, I break every vow, agreement, and programming*

connected to darkness, secrecy, and fear. I release this part
from all control and command every spiritual bondage to be
broken."

5. Deliverance as Led by the Spirit
Some parts may have demonic attachments. Never
confront demons for show. Ask Jesus to deal with them.
Once the part is ready, say: *"Jesus, would You take every*
unclean spirit that entered through this pain and command
them to leave now?"
Then ask the person if they see anything (like a cage or
chain) lifting or being removed. Many will visibly
describe what's happening.

6. Empower the Survivor
Many survivors feel powerless. Encourage them to make
choices. Let them choose if they're ready to forgive, to
integrate, or to trust Jesus. Never force. Honor the
process. Jesus is patient. We should be too.

Healing is Possible, Even After Ritual Abuse

One of the greatest lies survivors believe is: "I'm too broken.
I'll never be normal."
But here's the truth:

- You were never created to live in pieces.
- You are not too far gone.
- You are not forgotten.
- Your pain does not disqualify you from love.
- Jesus has already paid for your restoration—every
  part, every memory, every moment.

Healing may take time, but it is possible. I've walked with

people who thought they'd never sleep through the night, never trust again, never walk in freedom—and now they are whole, joyful, and ministering healing to others.

Jesus doesn't just bring comfort—He brings reconstruction. He restores what was stolen. He breaks what was built in darkness. He turns trauma into testimony.

Scripture as a Weapon in the Darkness

These are some powerful scriptures I speak and declare often in ministry to survivors:

- Isaiah 42:16 – *"I will lead the blind by ways they have not known... I will turn the darkness into light before them."* NIV
- Colossians 1:13 – *"He has rescued us from the dominion of darkness and brought us into the kingdom of the Son He loves."* NIV
- Psalm 91:4-6 – *"He will cover you with His feathers... You will not fear the terror of night."* NIV
- Romans 8:38-39 – *"Nothing can separate us from the love of God..."* NIV
- John 1:5 – *"The light shines in the darkness, and the darkness has not overcome it."* NIV

Use these as declarations. Post them. Pray them. Memorize them. They will anchor the soul when the darkness tries to pull someone back in.

A Final Word to the Survivor

If you are reading this and have survived ritual abuse, let me speak to your heart:

You are not alone.

You are not crazy.

You are not beyond repair.

You are brave.

You are worthy of love.

You are seen by God.

You are not what they said.

You are who Jesus says you are.

Let every programmed lie be exposed. Let every vow be broken. Let every part of you come out of hiding. Jesus is not afraid of the darkness you've walked through. He's not disgusted by what you carry. He doesn't run from pain. He runs to it.

And He's ready—right now—to begin the rescue.

To the Ministers and Intercessors

If God has called you to walk with survivors, you are on holy ground. Tread lightly, love deeply, and pray continually. You are not their Savior. Jesus is. But you are His hands, His voice, and His heart in the process.

Stay submitted. Stay humble. Stay filled with the Spirit.

And never forget—even ritual darkness must bow to the light of the risen King.

8

WHEN PARTS TURN DARK
UNDERSTANDING AND HEALING EVIL ALTERS

Some parts of the soul don't cry. They growl. Some don't beg for help. They fight it. Some don't respond to worship. They resist it. And when this happens in inner healing, many immediately assume, "This must be a demon."

But not everything that acts dark is demonic.

Sometimes, what you're dealing with is not a spirit from hell, but a part of a person's soul that has been so traumatized, twisted, and shaped by evil that it has taken on the identity of that darkness. These are what many call evil alters.

In this chapter, we will break down what evil alters are, how they are different from demons, how they form in the human soul, and how to bring these wounded, hostile parts into the light and love of Jesus Christ for redemption and healing. You will see that even the darkest parts of the soul are not beyond the reach of God's healing.

Understanding the Concept of an Evil Alter

To understand evil alters, we need to remember the biblical truth that the soul is complex. Scripture shows that the heart of man can hold good and evil, light and darkness, righteousness and iniquity. When trauma is severe and repeated, especially in the context of ritual abuse, demonic oppression, or violent upbringing, some soul fragments assume dark identities to survive.

These parts may:

- Take on names like "Death," "Destroyer," or "Punisher"
- Use violence or intimidation internally
- Curse God or hate anything spiritual
- Block healing and resist prayer
- Align with abusers or demonic ideologies

But they are still parts of the person—not external entities. They formed in darkness, but they are not beyond redemption.

An evil alter is a soul fragment that has made a covenant with darkness—believing lies, adopting evil roles, and agreeing with false identities. They are often formed during rituals, abuse, or prolonged trauma. Their purpose is to protect, punish, or preserve, even if it means partnering with evil.

Evil Alters vs. Demons: What's the Difference?

This distinction is critical. Demons are disembodied spirits with no human essence. Evil alters are wounded human soul parts.

Demons	Evil Altars
External spiritual beings	Internal soul fragments
Seek to torment or possess	Seek to protect, control or punish
Cast out by authority	Healed through love, truth, and Jesus' presence
No redemption possible	Fully redeemable and integrable
Oppose God's Kingdom	May have been taught to do so for survival

Trying to cast out an evil alter will often traumatize the person further, triggering more fragmentation and deepening the internal war. These parts need compassionate confrontation, truth-filled engagement, and Spirit-led healing, not aggressive deliverance.

How Evil Alters Are Formed

These parts form when pain is met with no relief, and fear is met with no comfort. Over time, the wounded soul may:

- Agree with darkness: "If I'm hated, I will become hate."
- Adopt an evil identity: "They called me a monster, so I'll be one."
- Bond with their abuser: A form of trauma bonding —"If I'm like them, I'll survive."
- Take vows of vengeance or silence: "I'll never trust again."
- Accept demonic lies as truth: "God hates me. I belong to Satan."

The enemy looks for these cracks—moments of despair, hatred, and rage—and inserts lies. If those lies are believed, parts of the soul may become hardened, isolated, or shaped by darkness.

But remember: these alters were not born evil. They were forged in pain. And what pain forged, Jesus can redeem.

Recognizing When You're Encountering an Evil Alter

Not every angry or resistant part is evil. But here are some signs you may be dealing with an evil alter:

- The part actively mocks or curses God
- The part expresses desire to harm the host or others
- The part claims to serve darkness or "belongs to the devil"
- The part says things like "I hate light," "I was created to destroy," or "I serve death"
- The part blocks other parts from coming forward
- The person feels intense fear, coldness, or oppression when this part surfaces

Don't panic. These are indicators that this part is in torment. And torment is the enemy's counterfeit throne. It is time for that throne to be torn down and replaced with truth.

Ministering to Evil Alters: Step by Step

Healing these parts takes deep spiritual sensitivity and authority. Here's a step-by-step model for walking with someone through this process:

1. Honor and Acknowledge the Part

Begin by speaking with respect, even if the part is hostile. Say something like: *"I know you've been protecting for a long time. I honor the role you've played, even if it was painful. You're not my enemy. You're a part of this person. I'd love to hear your story."*

Evil alters often expect to be rejected. Kindness disarms them.

2. Ask the Holy Spirit for Discernment

Ask: "Holy Spirit, is this a soul part or a demon?" Wait and listen. Many times, He will confirm in your spirit that this is a wounded part. Peace will come when you speak to them with truth.

3. Ask the Part Why It Was Created

This helps reveal the root. Questions like:
- "What happened to you?"
- "Why do you hate God?"
- "What were you told about yourself?"
- "Who told you your job was to destroy?"

These questions surface lies, trauma, and unmet needs.

4. Invite Jesus Into the Memory

Once the part reveals its pain, ask if Jesus can come. Say: "Jesus, will You come stand in this memory? Will You show this part who You really are?"

Let the person describe what they see. Often, Jesus appears to these parts as a warrior, rescuer, or judge—whatever they need most.

5. Ask Jesus to Speak the Truth

This is critical. Ask:

"Jesus, what do You want this part to know?"

Often, the part will hear something like:
"You are mine."
"You are not evil."
"You were never meant to carry this."
"You are forgiven."
"You are safe now."
Truth breaks the power of darkness.

6. Break Agreements and Renounce Darkness
Guide the part to say:
"I break agreement with darkness. I renounce every vow to evil. I choose truth. I choose Jesus."
Ask Jesus to cleanse this part with His blood. Invite the Holy Spirit to fill every space where darkness once ruled.

7. Invite Integration or Rest
Ask: "Would you like to come into the light? Would you like to be with the others?"
Some parts may integrate right away. Others may want to rest or stay close and watch. Follow their pace. Don't rush. Jesus is faithful to finish what He starts.

Stories of Redemption: From Darkness to Light

I've seen parts named "Death" become "Life."
I've seen parts that screamed curses begin to sing worship.
I've seen parts that served darkness become intercessors for light.

Here's one example:

A young woman came for ministry after years of suicidal thoughts, self-harm, and dissociation. As we prayed, a part surfaced named "Pain." This part hated God, hated people, and wanted to destroy the host. But as we engaged, the part told us it had been forced to participate in rituals as a child. It believed it belonged to Satan.

We invited Jesus. The room shifted. The part began to weep. "He's here," she said. "He's not afraid of me."

Jesus told that part, "You are not pain—you are precious."

That part renounced its allegiance to darkness, received forgiveness, and was wrapped in light. The girl described the part merging into her like warm oil. That day, a soul fragment was saved.

Jesus can do the same for anyone.

To the Evil Alter: You're Not Evil

If you're a part reading this—through the mind of the one you protect—hear me:
You are not the names they gave you.
You are not the role they forced on you.
You are not evil.
You are wounded. You are tired. You are loved.
You are a part of someone Jesus died for.
And He wants you—yes, you—to come home.

Let Him rename you. Let Him cleanse you. Let Him restore you.

Final Words to the Minister

When you encounter evil alters:

- Stay calm. You carry the Holy Spirit.
- Speak truth, not fear.
- Listen to Jesus more than the part.
- Always work toward redemption, not rejection.

You are not just casting out darkness—you are rescuing a captive.

You are not battling a foe—you are retrieving a family member of the soul.

Let the light of Christ shine into the darkest places. It always wins.

9

INHERITED PAIN

HEALING FROM INTERGENERATIONAL TRAUMA

There are wounds we can name—traumas we remember, events we survived, choices we made. But what do you do with pain that doesn't seem to have a source? What if your shame doesn't match your story? What if your fear seems older than you?

This is the mystery of intergenerational trauma—the reality that pain, dysfunction, and spiritual bondage don't begin with us, but they often live in us. They are passed down like heirlooms—unwanted, but familiar.

But the good news of the Kingdom is this: Jesus doesn't just heal what happened to you—He redeems what you inherited.

In this chapter, we'll explore the biblical foundation of generational patterns, how trauma is transmitted across family lines, the signs that you may be carrying inherited pain, and how to break cycles through repentance, renunciation, and legacy healing.

Biblical Foundations: Generational Blessings and Curses

From the very beginning, Scripture presents humanity not just as individuals, but as part of generational lines—family trees rooted in both blessing and consequence.

Exodus 20:5-6 says, *"I, the Lord your God, am a jealous God, punishing the children for the sin of the parents to the third and fourth generation... but showing love to a thousand generations of those who love Me and keep My commandments." NIV*

This is not about God being vindictive—it's about spiritual law. What is not healed or repented of in one generation creates access points for the next. It becomes a spiritual inheritance.

Generational curses are not arbitrary. They are the consequences of unrepented sin, trauma, idolatry, abuse, and occult involvement that open doors for demonic oppression or dysfunction across generations.

But generational blessing is also real. Every act of obedience, every surrender to Jesus, every breakthrough becomes seed for a different future. You are not just fighting for yourself —you are building legacy.

How Trauma Is Transmitted

Intergenerational trauma can be passed down through:

- Spiritual inheritance – unbroken curses, occult involvement, idolatry
- Biological inheritance – emotional reactivity, mental health predispositions

- Behavioral modeling – learned coping mechanisms, abuse cycles
- Family culture – silence, shame, secrecy, broken identity
- Unprocessed grief or rage – stored in the spiritual atmosphere of a home

For example:

- A grandfather who was rejected may become emotionally distant, causing his son to grow up with an orphan heart, who then raises his own children without affection.
- A mother involved in witchcraft may unknowingly open her bloodline to demonic oppression.
- An alcoholic father may never abuse his son, but the son still battles the same addiction without knowing why.

This is not about blame—it's about discernment. Jesus came to break cycles and start something new. But what is hidden must be brought into the light.

Signs of Intergenerational Trauma or Bondage

You may be dealing with inherited pain if:

- You feel deep shame, fear, or rage with no identifiable source
- Certain sins or dysfunctions run in the family (divorce, addiction, suicide, poverty, abuse)
- Your life seems to repeat your parents' or grandparents' pain

- You struggle with irrational self-hatred or fear of abandonment
- You feel cursed, trapped, or like you're fighting battles that aren't yours
- You have persistent dreams or inner images of family members connected to fear or control
- Occult, secret society, or false religion involvement appears in your family history

Inner healing is not only personal—it's intergenerational. You are the doorway through which God wants to heal your bloodline.

Spiritual Authority in the Bloodline

When you come into Christ, you are not just saved—you are authorized.

You now carry legal spiritual authority to break agreements made in your family line. What Jesus did on the cross wasn't just for you—it was to give you access to Heaven's courtroom, where you can renounce darkness and receive blessing.

"If anyone is in Christ, he is a new creation; the old has gone, the new is here." — 2 Corinthians 5:17 NIV

New creation means new identity, new inheritance, and new authority.

When you repent on behalf of your bloodline and renounce generational agreements, curses lose their legal right. Jesus stands as Advocate and Mediator, and His blood speaks a better word than any curse ever spoken.

The Process of Breaking Intergenerational Trauma

1. Ask the Holy Spirit to Reveal Patterns
Ask:

- "Holy Spirit, what generational pattern do You want to deal with?"
- "What was opened in my bloodline that I've carried unknowingly?"
- "Who in my family opened doors through sin or trauma?"

Let the Holy Spirit show you memories, dreams, or revelations about family history.

2. Repent on Behalf of the Bloodline
You are not taking blame—you are standing in the gap. Say something like:

"Father, I repent on behalf of my bloodline—for every sin, every agreement with darkness, every act of rebellion or idolatry. I plead the blood of Jesus over my generational line. I stand in the authority of Christ to break these cycles and invite Your cleansing."

3. Renounce Generational Agreements
Speak it out loud. Name what God reveals.

"In the name of Jesus, I break every generational curse of fear, shame, addiction, control, poverty, and rejection. I renounce every agreement with darkness made by my ancestors—known or unknown. I break all ties to witchcraft, idolatry, and perversion. I declare those doors are closed in Jesus' name."

4. Forgive Those Who Passed It Down
Even if it was unconscious or unintentional, release them.

"I forgive my father, mother, grandparents, and ancestors for what they passed on. I release them from blame. I bless them, and I receive the mercy of God for my family."

Forgiveness unblocks inheritance.

5. Invite Jesus to Establish Legacy Blessing
This is more than breaking—this is building.

"Jesus, I invite You to release generational blessing over me and my descendants. I receive a new inheritance—of peace, intimacy, purpose, and joy. I declare that I am a cycle-breaker and a legacy builder in the Kingdom of God."

Ask the Lord:

- What blessing are You giving me to pass on?
- What new name, role, or anointing are You establishing in my family line?

He will often speak directly to identity and destiny in this moment.

Healing for Your Generations — Before and After You

This is not just about you being healed. It's about healing those who came before you—and blessing those who come after.

Through the Spirit, you can even minister healing to family

members who are no longer alive. No, we don't talk to the dead. But we do release forgiveness, blessing, and spiritual cleansing over the past.

And we certainly build for the future.

Your healing sets a new precedent:

- Your children won't grow up with what you fought through.
- Your grandchildren will walk in blessings you didn't even know existed.
- Your name will be spoken in Heaven as a turning point in your bloodline.

Legacy Declarations

Speak these out over yourself:

- I am the first in my family to walk in freedom from fear.
- I am not repeating the pain of my parents—I am rewriting the story.
- Every curse ends with me. Every blessing begins with me.
- I am adopted into the family of God—His blood defines my inheritance.
- My ceiling will be my children's floor.
- I will leave a legacy of righteousness, joy, and peace.

Prayers of Legacy Healing

Prayer of Identification and Repentance:

Father, I come before You on behalf of my family line. I identify the sins, traumas, and agreements made that opened doors to darkness. I repent for all generational involvement in idolatry, witchcraft, abuse, addiction, immorality, hatred, control, and pride. I ask You to cleanse my bloodline by the blood of Jesus.

Prayer of Renunciation:

In the name of Jesus, I renounce every generational curse and all demonic inheritance. I break agreement with shame, fear, confusion, perversion, and torment. I cancel every word curse and vow spoken over me and my family. I declare that I am no longer under the authority of darkness. I belong to the Kingdom of Light.

Prayer of Blessing and Legacy:

Lord, I receive Your blessing upon me and my family. I receive the full inheritance of Your Kingdom. Let my children and grandchildren walk in greater freedom than I've known. Let the legacy of my family be changed by Your mercy and power. Let my story be redemption, restoration, and generational joy.

You Were Born to Break Cycles

You are not weak—you are a warrior.
You are not cursed—you are called.
You are not your ancestors—you are anointed.
And you are not alone.

Jesus stands with you—Sword in hand, blood on the mercy seat, and love in His eyes. He is the Breaker of Chains, the Restorer of Generations, the One who rewrites family lines.

You are His chosen vessel for a new legacy.

You are the turning point.

10

PRESENTING JESUS
A SPIRIT-LED MODEL OF INNER HEALING
AND DELIVERANCE

There's a sacred moment when someone closes their eyes, asks the Holy Spirit to reveal a wound, and a memory surfaces—a moment of pain buried deep but not forgotten. The air thickens. Tears brim. And then we say the words: "Can I invite Jesus into that memory?"

The atmosphere changes.
He enters.
And everything begins to shift.

This is the heartbeat of the Presenting Jesus model—a Spirit-led, trauma-informed, Kingdom-based approach to inner healing and deliverance where the wounded meet the Healer in the very place they were hurt.

This chapter will unpack this process—one that has become a sacred rhythm in the healing journey of many, including those at SOZO Church and beyond. While influenced by models such as Theophostic Prayer Ministry, Heart-

Sync, and the Immanuel Approach, this model is rooted in the simplicity of encountering Jesus personally, hearing His voice, and walking into freedom.

Why Presenting Jesus Works

Jesus is not just a theological concept—He's a living Person. And He is the One who heals the brokenhearted (Luke 4:18). He is the Lamb who was slain and the Good Shepherd who gathers fragments and restores the soul.

We don't just talk about Jesus—we invite Him into memories. We don't just tell people God loves them—we watch Him prove it in real-time as He walks into their pain.

This method is grounded in:

- John 14:18 — *"I will not leave you as orphans; I will come to you."* NIV
- Psalm 34:18 — *"The Lord is close to the brokenhearted."* NIV
- Revelation 3:20 — *"I stand at the door and knock. If anyone hears My voice and opens the door, I will come in..."* NKJV
- Hebrews 13:8 — *"Jesus Christ is the same yesterday, today, and forever."* NKJV

This isn't imagination—it's invitation.
Not visualization—visitation.
The living Jesus shows up in wounds and makes them whole.

Step 1: Invite the Holy Spirit to Reveal a Wound

Every healing session begins with honoring the Holy Spirit as the Guide.

"Holy Spirit, will You bring to mind a memory—a moment in their life—where their heart was wounded and has not yet been healed?"

The person usually closes their eyes and quietly waits. A memory may come instantly, or after a few moments. Often, it is accompanied by emotion: tears, tension, or physical sensation.

When a memory arises, the person gives a simple nod or verbal confirmation:

"Yes, I have one."

We don't probe, push, or pry. We wait for the wound the Holy Spirit chooses to surface.

Step 2: Explore the Memory Gently

Ask:

- "Where are you in this memory?"
- "Who is with you?"
- "What is happening?"

Let them describe it in their own words. You're not there to fix or interpret. You're there to listen with love and guide with discernment.

Ask:

- "What are you feeling in this moment?"

- "What are you believing about yourself, about others, or about God right now?"

This is where lies are often uncovered:

- "I'm not safe."
- "I'm unlovable."
- "It's my fault."
- "God wasn't there."
- "I'm alone."

These lies become spiritual strongholds. But lies can't live in the presence of Truth. And Truth is about to walk in.

Step 3: Invite Jesus into the Memory

This is the moment everything changes.

Say: "If it's okay with you, can I invite Jesus to come into this memory?"

Wait for their yes. Then pray:

"Jesus, would You come into this memory right now—just as You are. Show Yourself to this person. Let them see where You are. Let them know You are here."

Pause. Give the person space to experience His presence. Ask:

- "Can you see Him?"
- "Where is He in the memory?"
- "What is He doing?"
- "How do you feel now that He's here?"

This is where awe enters the room. Jesus is not passive—He moves, speaks, shields, embraces, weeps, defends, restores.

Wounds that felt overwhelming are suddenly overshadowed by His presence. Fear begins to break. Truth begins to be spoken.

Step 4: Let Jesus Confront the Lies

Ask Jesus directly—out loud if needed:
"Jesus, [Name] believes they're not worthy. Is that true?"

Then ask the person:
"What is Jesus saying in response?"

Jesus will speak truth:

- "You are My beloved."
- "You were never alone."
- "It wasn't your fault."
- "I've always been with you."

These words are not generic—they are surgical, personal, and liberating.

When Jesus speaks, strongholds begin to crumble. A single phrase from the mouth of the Healer heals what years of striving could not.

Step 5: Walk Through Forgiveness

Now that safety and truth are present, forgiveness can flow.
Ask: *"Jesus, is there anyone in this memory [Name] needs to forgive?"*

He often reveals the one who caused the pain. Sometimes it's a parent, an abuser, a friend. Sometimes it's God. Sometimes it's themselves.

Ask:

- "Are you willing to forgive them with Jesus' help?"
- "Would you like to tell them you forgive them now?"

If they can't, ask Jesus to show them the brokenness of that person. Compassion often leads the way to forgiveness.

Then have them say: *"I forgive you. I release you. You no longer owe me anything."*

This is not condoning the action. It's cutting the tie that kept them bound to the pain.

Step 6: Release the Protector and Integrate the Wounded Part

Sometimes in the memory, a part of them is still stuck. A protector may appear—angry, controlling, numb, or defensive.

Say: *"Speak to the protector part. Tell them: 'You don't have to protect me anymore. Jesus is here now.'"*

Then say: *"Jesus, will You take this protector and bring them into Your care?"*

Next, bring the healed adult self into the memory.

Say: *"See yourself at your current age step into that memory.*

Speak to the younger version of you. What do you want to say? What comfort can you offer?"

Then ask: *"Can you give that younger part a hug? Can you invite that part to come into the present with you and be healed?"*

Often, the person sees the younger part grow and merge with them—symbolizing healing and integration.

Step 7: Cast Out Any Attached Spirits

Some wounds become landing strips for demonic oppression. If evil spirits entered through trauma, rejection, fear, or occult involvement, this is the moment to deal with them.

Ask: *"Jesus, are there any spirits that entered through this wound?"*

Then command: *"In the name of Jesus, I command every spirit attached to this wound to go into the cage. You no longer have access."*

Ask the person: *"Do you see the cage?"*

Many see it and describe what spirits are there (shame, fear, self-hatred, etc.)

Then declare: *"Jesus, we ask You to take that cage to the pit. Every spirit must go where You send them."*

Then seal the moment: *"I command every evil spirit to leave now and never return. This person is covered by the blood of Jesus. Amen."*

Step 8: Ask Jesus for the Gift of Exchange

Jesus never just takes pain—He gives beauty in its place.

Ask: *"Jesus, is there anything You want to give [Name] in exchange for what was taken?"*

Often, He gives a new name, a robe, a crown, a scroll, or simply says, "I love you."

These gifts become anchors for identity. They are sacred.

Then say: *"See you and Jesus walking out of the memory together."*

That memory is now healed ground. It no longer holds trauma—it holds testimony.

Comparison with Other Spirit-Led Models

Theophostic Prayer focuses on lies formed in traumatic experiences and invites Jesus' truth.

The Immanuel Approach builds from relational connection and emotional attunement with Jesus.

HeartSync engages fragmented parts (Function, Emotion, Guardian) for deep integration and connection.

Presenting Jesus stands on similar foundations but emphasizes simplicity, real-time interaction, and a seamless flow between healing, deliverance, forgiveness, and integration.

It is relational, Holy Spirit-led, and deeply rooted in Kingdom authority and compassion.

Why This Matters

People don't need clever words or religious formulas.
They need Jesus to walk into their story.
They need His voice to shatter the lies.
They need His eyes to see them.
They need His presence in their pain.

That's what this model offers. Not just a method—but a meeting place. Not just a framework—but freedom.

11

JESUS THE HEALER
WHAT SCRIPTURE SAYS ABOUT INNER HEALING

Before Jesus ever cast out a demon, walked on water, or rose from the dead, He stood in a synagogue in Nazareth, unrolling the scroll of Isaiah. The words He read would become the mission statement of His ministry:

> *"The Spirit of the Lord is upon Me, because He has anointed Me to preach good news to the poor. He has sent Me to heal the brokenhearted..."*
> —Luke 4:18 NKJV

Jesus came for the wounded.

He didn't just come to take sin to the cross—He came to bring healing to the soul. The brokenness of humanity, from the inside out, was always part of what He came to restore. He didn't separate salvation from healing, because the Father never did. Wholeness was always the plan.

The Healing Jesus We Often Overlook

In many circles, Jesus is primarily preached as the Savior from sin. And He is. But if we only see Him as the One who saves us from something, we miss that He also saves us into something: wholeness, fullness, and restoration.

Jesus didn't walk the earth looking only for people to forgive—He came looking for people to heal. Everywhere He went, He mended what was broken—bodies, souls, identities, relationships, reputations, even communities.

He didn't just tell the woman with the issue of blood, "Your sins are forgiven." He said, "Daughter, your faith has healed you. Go in peace and be freed from your suffering" (Mark 5:34). That moment wasn't just a medical miracle—it was a soul restoration. She was publicly shamed and privately bleeding. But when Jesus touched her, she was called "daughter," healed in body, and restored in identity.

Jesus doesn't just heal sickness. He heals suffering. That includes emotional trauma, inner torment, and broken hearts.

A Biblical Theology of Wholeness

The biblical word for healing in many New Testament passages is "sozo." It means more than physical healing—it means salvation, deliverance, protection, and wholeness. When Jesus healed, forgave, and delivered, it was all part of the same mission. He was revealing the heart of the Father to make His children whole again.

"Go," Jesus told the woman caught in adultery, "and sin no more." But before that, He gave her dignity, protection, and identity.

"He has borne our griefs and carried our sorrows..." (Isaiah 53:4, NKJV)

"By His wounds, we are healed." (Isaiah 53:5 ESV)

The stripes Jesus bore were not only for the healing of physical bodies—but for the wounding of souls.

The Psalmist wrote:

"He heals the brokenhearted and binds up their wounds." (Psalm 147:3) NKJV

That's not poetic exaggeration—it's divine truth.

Jesus and the Emotionally Wounded

The Gospels are filled with stories of people whose pain was more emotional than physical:

- The woman at the well — rejected, isolated, and shame-filled (John 4). Jesus didn't touch her body— He touched her story.
- The demonized man in the tombs — tormented, isolated, self-harming (Mark 5). Jesus not only cast out the legion, He clothed him, restored his mind, and commissioned his voice.
- Peter — after denying Jesus, was restored not by rebuke but by breakfast, friendship, and three invitations to love again (John 21).
- Mary Magdalene — out of whom Jesus cast seven demons, became the first evangelist of the resurrection (Luke 8:2, John 20:18).

Healing always leads to purpose. Restoration always precedes mission.

The Healing Mission of Jesus: A Summary from the Gospels

- He healed the sick (Matthew 4:24; Mark 1:32-34)
- He cleansed lepers — restoring dignity and access to community (Luke 17:11-19)
- He raised the dead — confronting the finality of loss with resurrection power (John 11)
- He opened blind eyes and unstopped deaf ears — restoring senses, but also spiritual discernment (Mark 10, Luke 7)
- He cast out demons — bringing deliverance from torment (Mark 5, Luke 4)
- He forgave sins — linking sin and sickness but not always conflating them (Luke 5:17-26)
- He restored relationships — Zacchaeus, Peter, the woman caught in adultery (Luke 19, John 8)

Inner Healing as Part of Salvation

In the Western Church, salvation is often reduced to a moment—a prayer or decision. But in Scripture, salvation (sozo) is a holistic restoration. It involves healing from sin's effects on the spirit, soul, and body.

> *"May your whole spirit, soul, and body be kept blameless at the coming of our Lord Jesus Christ."* (1 Thess. 5:23) NIV

Jesus is not content to have only your spirit go to Heaven. He wants your soul to be healed on the way there.

When He said, *"Come to Me all who are weary and burdened, and I will give you rest"* (Matthew 11:28), He was not giving a theology of rest—He was offering a healing place for the tormented heart.

Healing the Soul: Jesus' Encounters with the Broken

Let's revisit some key moments of Jesus' healing ministry that reveal His heart for inner healing.

1. The Woman with the Alabaster Jar (Luke 7:36–50)
She wept at His feet. She was forgiven. But more than that, she was seen. Jesus acknowledged her love, not her sin. Her story is about freedom from shame.

2. The Paralytic Lowered Through the Roof (Luke 5:17–26)
Before Jesus healed his body, He said, "Your sins are forgiven." The crowd was confused, but Jesus revealed a truth: Healing of the soul often precedes healing of the body.

3. The Gadarene Demoniac (Mark 5:1–20)
He was naked, isolated, and cutting himself. After meeting Jesus, he was "clothed, in his right mind," and sent as a messenger of hope. This is a picture of deliverance, healing, and reintegration of identity.

Jesus Still Heals Today

Hebrews 13:8 says: *"Jesus Christ is the same yesterday, today, and forever."* NKJV

The healing Jesus of the Gospels is still healing today. He

does it through the presence of the Holy Spirit, the ministry of His people, and moments where He walks right into someone's story and speaks one word: "Peace."

If Jesus is still the same, then His mission hasn't changed. And if His mission hasn't changed, then healing is still part of the Gospel. Inner healing is not optional for some—it is essential for all.

Healing as an Invitation to Know Him

Ultimately, healing is not about escaping pain—it's about encountering the Healer.

"He was despised and rejected—a man of sorrows, acquainted with grief..." (Isaiah 53:3 NKJV)

Jesus knows what it's like to be wounded, betrayed, abandoned, and misunderstood. That's why He walks so tenderly into our wounds—He's been there too.

Every time we invite Him into a wound, we don't just experience healing—we experience Him.

Responding to the Healing Jesus

As you read this, pause and ask:

- What part of my heart still needs healing?
- What lie am I believing about God, myself, or others?
- Where have I hidden my pain instead of inviting Jesus in?

Then pray:

"Jesus, You are the Healer. You didn't just come to save me from sin, but to make me whole. I invite You into my broken places. Speak Your truth. Restore my soul. Amen."

12

THE HOLY SPIRIT AND INNER HEALING

There is no true healing without the Holy Spirit. He is the active, intimate presence of God at work in the human heart—mending what is broken, restoring what is lost, and leading us back to the Father's original design for our lives. The Spirit is not distant, passive, or abstract. He is a person—divine and deeply present—who walks with us into the darkest wounds and the deepest memories, not to shame us, but to liberate us. Inner healing, at its core, is not just about resolving emotional pain; it is about encounter—encountering the Comforter in the places we've tried to hide or forget.

This chapter will explore the indispensable role of the Holy Spirit in inner healing, and how learning to partner with Him is key to walking in sustained freedom and wholeness.

The Comforter: God's Healing Presence in Pain

When Jesus promised the Holy Spirit, He referred to Him as the Comforter (John 14:16 KJV). That word in Greek is Parakletos—meaning one who comes alongside to help, to advocate, to encourage. The very nature of the Holy Spirit is to draw close to the afflicted and speak peace to the tormented. The enemy often convinces people in pain that they are alone, abandoned, or unworthy of love. But the Comforter enters gently, persistently, and with supernatural compassion.

In ministry sessions, I've seen the moment the Comforter shows up in someone's wound. Their whole countenance shifts —sometimes with tears, sometimes with a sense of lightness or calm that floods the soul. When the Holy Spirit is present, the pain doesn't just get managed—it gets met with love. That's when transformation begins.

Ask the Holy Spirit to show you the places where you still need comfort. Invite Him not as a visitor, but as a healer, to dwell in those areas. You don't need to pretend for Him. He already knows—and He comes with oil, not stones.

The Counselor: Wisdom and Strategy in Healing

The Holy Spirit is also our Counselor (Isaiah 11:2; John 14:26). He doesn't just soothe our wounds—He knows the exact path to wholeness. When ministering inner healing, we cannot rely on formulas or scripts. Each person's soul is different. Trauma doesn't unfold in linear patterns. That's why partnering with the Spirit is critical—He custom-designs each healing encounter.

There have been countless times when I paused during a session to ask, "Holy Spirit, what are You doing right now?" And then the direction shifts—He highlights a childhood memory, or a hidden vow, or a lie rooted in shame. Without His counsel, we might address symptoms and miss the root. But the

Counselor sees the whole soul map, and He leads us gently but thoroughly.

If you're ministering healing to others—or seeking it yourself—learn to pause and ask, "What do You see that I don't? What do You want to do here?" His voice will never condemn you, but He will convict, clarify, and lead you into truth.

The Revealer: Exposing Hidden Wounds and Lies

The Holy Spirit is also the Spirit of Truth (John 16:13). Inner healing involves surfacing the hidden lies we have believed—about ourselves, about God, and about others. Many of these lies are embedded in traumatic memories, where pain distorted reality. A child abused by a parent may conclude, "I'm unlovable," or "I must protect myself or I'll be hurt again." These lies shape identity and behavior—but they are not the truth.

Only the Holy Spirit can expose these lies with tenderness and clarity. He doesn't rip off bandages to embarrass; He uncovers wounds to cleanse. As the Revealer, He brings memories to the surface—not to re-traumatize us, but to heal us. He points out strongholds, soul ties, and false beliefs—not with accusation, but with the invitation to be free.

In sessions, I often ask, "Holy Spirit, what lie did they believe in that moment?" and "Jesus, what do You want them to know instead?" His answers dismantle years of torment in a moment. Truth heals what time cannot.

The Restorer: Bringing Integration and Wholeness

Finally, the Holy Spirit is our Restorer. He doesn't just take away pain—He restores what was stolen. Joel 2:25 says, "I will restore to you the years the locust has eaten." That's not just poetic—it's prophetic. Restoration is the heart of the Spirit's work. He brings back joy, trust, purity, purpose, and presence to places we thought were permanently damaged.

This restoration often looks like integration—bringing scattered parts of the soul back together. A person who has lived fragmented through trauma begins to feel whole again. They start to recognize themselves. They regain access to memories, emotions, and functions that were once locked away. This is not psychology alone—it is the power of the Holy Spirit renewing the mind and soul.

Restoration also means replanting purpose. Many people who go through inner healing say, "I feel like I'm becoming who I was always meant to be." That's because the Holy Spirit doesn't just remove pain—He reawakens destiny.

Partnering with the Spirit in Ministry

As you grow in inner healing, whether receiving it or ministering it, your relationship with the Holy Spirit must deepen. Invite Him into every moment. Ask Him for discernment, wisdom, and love. Don't rush or assume—learn His flow.

Here are some practical ways to partner with the Holy Spirit in inner healing:

1. Ask Him to guide the session — Begin every time of ministry with prayer. Invite Him to be the leader, not just the helper.
2. Tune your ears to His voice — His nudges may come through Scripture, impressions, pictures, or a still small voice.

3. Follow His peace — If you feel a check or lack of peace, pause. He may be redirecting you.
4. Yield to His timing — Some healing comes quickly, other parts take process. Trust His wisdom.
5. Worship as warfare — Invite the Spirit to fill the space with His presence. Worship opens the soul.
6. Stay humble — You are not the healer. He is. Your job is obedience, not performance.

The Spirit Is Still Speaking

We must never forget—this isn't just theory. The Holy Spirit is still speaking. He is still healing. He is still moving. He wants to work through you—and in you.

You do not need to be a trained therapist to help others find healing. You need to be Spirit-led, surrendered, and loving. The Spirit will do the heavy lifting.

And for those still walking through your own pain: the Spirit has not forgotten you. He is with you. He is for you. He is within you. And He is leading you into wholeness that only Heaven can author.

The Holy Spirit is not just part of the process—He is the process. Healing is not possible without Him. But with Him, all things are possible.

13

FORGIVENESS: THE GATE TO FREEDOM

T here are few words in the Kingdom of God as powerful, misunderstood, and resisted as forgiveness. It is the divine hinge on which inner healing swings. Without forgiveness, the door to wholeness remains bolted shut. With it, what was once locked behind bitterness, trauma, and pain swings wide open to light, freedom, and joy. This chapter explores why forgiveness is not just a recommendation—it's a commandment, a key, and a Kingdom weapon of deliverance and healing.

1. Why Forgiveness Unlocks Healing

Forgiveness is the spiritual scalpel that cuts away infection in the soul. When we carry bitterness, resentment, and offense, we tether ourselves to the very pain we long to be free from. In Matthew 18:34-35, Jesus tells the parable of the unforgiving servant and says the man was handed over to the tormentors until he forgave his brother from the heart. Unforgiveness is not just a moral issue—it becomes a spiritual stronghold where torment, oppression, and emotional bondage dwell.

When we forgive, we aren't pretending the pain didn't happen. We're choosing to release someone from the debt they owe us—so that we can walk out of the prison ourselves.

Forgiveness doesn't make what was done right—it makes us free.

2. What Forgiveness Is and What It Is Not

Too often, people avoid forgiveness because they believe it means excusing or justifying wrongdoing. But forgiveness does not say:

- "What happened didn't matter."
- "I have to trust this person again."
- "It's all okay now."

Forgiveness does say:

- "I choose to release the offense to God."
- "I give up the right to punish."
- "I refuse to let bitterness take root."

Forgiveness is not reconciliation. It is not denying or forgetting. It is not the absence of consequences. It is a spiritual transaction where we surrender the burden of justice to the Lord and let Him be the righteous Judge.

3. Forgiving Others — Letting Go of the Offense

When someone wounds us—especially someone close—the offense can go deep. Their betrayal, neglect, or abuse doesn't just touch the emotions. It embeds itself in the soul. We replay what they said. We feel it in our bodies. And we often create entire inner worlds (protector parts, lies, vows) around never being hurt again.

Forgiveness begins when we face the pain and choose to give it to Jesus. This often means walking back into memories, not to relive the trauma, but to invite the Healer into it. We name what they did. We feel what it cost. Then we say the words that break the chain: "I choose to forgive them for..."

Some wounds require repeating this process many times. Forgiveness is a process that often starts with a decision and is followed by repeated alignment of the heart.

Forgiveness doesn't always feel fair. But neither did the cross.

Jesus absorbed the ultimate injustice so we could walk in undeserved mercy—and extend that same mercy to others.

4. Forgiving Yourself — Receiving Grace You Didn't Earn

For many, the hardest person to forgive is not an abuser, a parent, or a betrayer. It's themselves. Shame is one of the enemy's favorite prisons, and self-hatred becomes the jailer. People blame themselves for trauma they endured. They carry guilt for choices they made. They wish they had acted differently. And in the absence of grace, they torment themselves with silent accusations.

But if the blood of Jesus was enough for God to forgive you—who are you to withhold forgiveness from yourself?

Self-forgiveness is not minimizing sin or denying mistakes. It is saying, "I no longer agree with the accuser. I agree with the blood of Jesus." It is letting the truth of the gospel sink so deep that even your shame has to bow. It is giving yourself the same mercy God already extended.

Many inner healing encounters are blocked because the person refuses to receive what they freely offer others—grace.

If you wouldn't speak to someone else the way you speak to yourself, it's time to forgive yourself.

5. Reconciling with God — Releasing Blame, Embracing Truth

Though few admit it, many believers carry disappointment or anger toward God. In moments of pain, especially childhood trauma, the question arises: Where were You, God? The enemy rushes in with lies: "God let it happen. He didn't care. He's not safe."

These false beliefs become internal wounds. And though theologically we know God is perfect, our hearts may still hold Him at a distance.

True healing requires letting God speak for Himself.

This does not mean God needs forgiveness in the sense of wrongdoing—He never sins. But we often need to release the pain we aimed at Him. We confess the lies we believed, renounce judgments we've made against Him, and allow His love to show us where He was all along.
This process often includes:

- Confessing where we've blamed God

- Asking Him to reveal the truth about those moments
- Choosing to trust His nature again

God is not afraid of your questions. He desires reconciliation and is eager to restore intimacy.

6. The Fruit of Forgiveness — Peace, Power, and Presence

When people truly forgive, the change is tangible. They often experience physical relief, emotional clarity, and a new sensitivity to the Holy Spirit. The bitterness that once clouded their discernment lifts. Their bodies stop holding tension. Their faces soften. Their joy returns.

Forgiveness makes room for God to dwell. His presence increases where judgment, bitterness, and pain once lived. What once echoed with torment now sings with peace.

Some benefits of forgiveness include:

- Freedom from demonic torment
- Emotional lightness and clarity
- Restored intimacy with God
- Reopened hearts for relationships
- Physical healing (many illnesses are tied to bitterness)

Forgiveness is not weakness—it's spiritual warfare. It is disarming the enemy by taking away his access. It is closing the door on darkness and opening the windows to light.

7. Forgiveness and Inner Healing Prayer

Here is a model prayer to guide someone into forgiveness:

"Father, I come to You in the name of Jesus. I choose to forgive [name the person] for [specifically name what they did], even though it hurt and wounded me deeply. I release them from the debt they owe me. I choose to let go of the pain, anger, and desire for revenge. I ask You to take the burden from me and heal the wound in my heart.
If I've blamed You, God, for what happened, I release that judgment now and ask for Your truth to flood my heart. I also choose to forgive myself for [what I've done or believed], and I receive Your grace. I break all agreement with shame, guilt, and condemnation. Holy Spirit, come and fill every place where pain and bitterness once lived. Thank You for the cross. Thank You for mercy. Thank You for freedom. In Jesus' name, amen."

This prayer is not magical—but it is powerful when partnered with a surrendered heart.

8. Living a Lifestyle of Forgiveness

Jesus told Peter to forgive not seven times, but seventy times seven (Matthew 18:22). Why? Because forgiveness isn't a one-time act—it's a way of living.

To live healed, we must live forgiving. Every day brings new opportunities to be offended, overlooked, or hurt. But with each opportunity comes the invitation: Will you choose freedom again?

Living a lifestyle of forgiveness means:

- We keep short accounts with others
- We speak truth and release offense quickly
- We guard our hearts from bitterness
- We partner with Heaven's justice, not our own

Forgiveness doesn't always end in restored relationship.

Some boundaries are necessary. But it always results in restored freedom—within us.

9. Forgiveness in Community — Building a Culture of Mercy

When entire families, churches, or teams embrace forgiveness, a new atmosphere is born—one where vulnerability thrives, love flows freely, and reconciliation becomes normal.

Communities built on unforgiveness are heavy, divided, and spiritually dry. But those built on mercy become places where the Spirit of God dwells.

You can help build a culture of forgiveness by:

- Modeling it publicly and privately
- Teaching it as part of discipleship
- Praying for it regularly in your environment
- Calling people out of offense with love and truth

When forgiveness becomes normal, so does healing.

10. The Cross — Our Ultimate Model and Motivation

At the center of forgiveness is the cross. Jesus didn't just teach forgiveness—He became it. With blood running down His face, breath fading from His lungs, and nails piercing His flesh, He looked at His murderers and said, *"Father, forgive them, for they do not know what they do"* (Luke 23:34 NKJV).

There is no greater power than that kind of love.

You forgive not because they deserve it—but because you were forgiven. You release the debt not because it cost nothing, but because Jesus paid it all.

Forgiveness is not just a Kingdom tool—it is a Kingdom culture. A forgiven people become a forgiving people. A healed person becomes a healer. And a life shaped by mercy becomes a life that sets others free.

You don't have to carry that pain any longer.
The gate is open.
The key is in your hand.
It's time to forgive—and walk into freedom.

Let the healing begin.

14

THE POWER OF VOWS
IDENTIFYING AND BREAKING INNER VOWS

The Hidden Agreements That Shape Our Lives

Some of the most binding chains we carry are the ones we forge ourselves. These chains are not physical, but spiritual and emotional—rooted in words we've spoken in pain, disappointment, and fear. "I'll never trust anyone again." "I'll always be alone." "I'll never let anyone get close." These phrases may seem like harmless expressions of frustration, but they are often inner vows—deep, soul-level agreements we make to protect ourselves, which end up imprisoning us.

Inner vows form when we experience pain, betrayal, trauma, or shame, and we try to seize control of our lives through self-protection. While the vow may seem like a survival instinct, it actually becomes a spiritual agreement that binds us to fear, isolation, and lies. In this chapter, we will explore how inner vows form, how they block intimacy and hinder healing, and how to break them by aligning with God's truth.

What Are Inner Vows?

An inner vow is a self-made promise or declaration we make in our hearts, often during a moment of deep pain or trauma. Unlike intentional oaths, these vows are subconscious commitments we make in response to fear, disappointment, or broken trust. They typically sound like:

- "I will never be like my father."
- "No one will ever hurt me again."
- "I can only depend on myself."
- "I'll never show emotion again."

These vows are not merely emotional reactions; they are spiritual contracts. They operate beneath the surface of our awareness, shaping our decisions, relationships, and responses to life. They can lock us into cycles of fear, perfectionism, independence, emotional coldness, or control.

Scripture warns us about the power of the tongue and the significance of our declarations. Proverbs 18:21 says, *"Death and life are in the power of the tongue, and those who love it will eat its fruit."* Inner vows align us with death—not literal physical death, but the spiritual death of connection, vulnerability, trust, and freedom.

How Inner Vows Form

Inner vows are often formed in childhood or adolescence when our capacity to process pain is undeveloped. A child raised in a chaotic or abusive home may inwardly vow, "I will never need anyone." A girl rejected by her father may vow, "I won't trust men." A boy bullied for crying may vow, "I'll never show weakness again."

These vows are our soul's attempt to gain control over what hurt us. But they don't actually protect us—they imprison us. The moment we make the vow, we shift from trusting God as our defender to trusting ourselves as the one who must manage pain. This shift is spiritual. It opens the door to strongholds of fear, pride, isolation, and control.

Because vows are tied to pain, they are usually reinforced over time. We interpret new experiences through the lens of the vow: when someone disappoints us, we remember the vow and tighten its grip. It becomes our default lens and a false comforter. But the Holy Spirit was sent to be our Comforter and Guide, not fear, self-protection, or inner vows.

The Fruit of Inner Vows

The fruit of inner vows is often hidden but always toxic. Here are common manifestations:

- Control Issues: The vow says, "No one will hurt me again," so you micromanage your life and others to stay safe.
- Emotional Walls: You struggle to be vulnerable because you vowed never to feel weak again.
- Perfectionism: A vow to never fail creates a deep drive to be flawless, fueled by fear of shame.
- Isolation: A vow to never trust again leads to loneliness and guarded relationships.
- Performance-Based Identity: A vow to never be like a parent who failed you leads to living for approval instead of grace.
- Distrust of Authority: A vow to never be controlled again results in resistance to leaders or mentors, even godly ones.

These fruits seem like personality traits or quirks, but they are often symptoms of a spiritual agreement that must be broken.

Why Inner Vows Block Intimacy and Healing

Inner vows block intimacy because they build walls where God wants to build bridges. When we say "I'll never need anyone," we block the flow of love, support, and connection. When we say "I'll never trust again," we make trust impossible —even when it's safe and God-ordained. These vows keep us in survival mode, not sonship. They block the vulnerability required for healthy community, marriage, and even our relationship with God.

Moreover, inner vows block healing because they are rooted in agreement with lies. Healing requires truth. Inner vows are self-constructed, flesh-driven attempts to protect ourselves, but Jesus is our Shepherd and Protector. Until we renounce the vow, we are trying to heal while still holding onto the mechanism that caused the wound to fester. You cannot be healed while still clinging to the weapon that cut you.

Biblical Examples and Principles

Though Scripture doesn't use the phrase "inner vow," it is filled with examples of the power of the heart's commitments and spoken words:

- Jephthah's vow (Judges 11:30–39): He made a rash vow that led to deep sorrow.
- Peter's vow (Matthew 26:35): *"Even if I have to die with you, I will never disown you."* He made a vow rooted in pride, not revelation, and broke it.

- Ecclesiastes 5:4–6 warns: *"When you make a vow to God, do not delay to fulfill it. He has no pleasure in fools; fulfill your vow… Do not let your mouth lead you into sin." NIV*

While these speak of vows made to God, the principle remains: vows are weighty and shape the course of our lives. Jesus warned us to let our "Yes" be yes and our "No" be no, because anything beyond that comes from the evil one (Matthew 5:37). Inner vows often go beyond what is simple and true—they are fueled by fear, pride, and pain.

How to Break Inner Vows

Breaking inner vows is a spiritual and emotional process. It requires the Holy Spirit's illumination, honesty about the pain that birthed the vow, and a willing heart to exchange self-protection for God's protection. Here are the steps:

1. Ask the Holy Spirit to Reveal Any Inner Vows
Prayerfully invite the Lord to show you where you've made vows. He may bring to mind phrases you've said or attitudes that reflect a vow. Journaling can help surface patterns. Ask, "Holy Spirit, are there any promises I made to myself that are blocking Your truth?"

2. Identify the Root Pain or Trauma
Where did the vow begin? What pain were you trying to avoid? Bring that memory or moment before the Lord. Often it's tied to rejection, abuse, abandonment, shame, or betrayal.

3. Repent for Making the Vow
Inner vows are acts of self-reliance. Repent for trusting yourself over God. Confess the vow and renounce it aloud. For example: "Lord, I repent for the vow I made that I would never need anyone. I break agreement with that lie in Jesus' name."

4. Forgive Those Who Hurt You
Inner vows are often tied to unforgiveness. Forgiveness doesn't justify the hurt; it sets you free. Say: "I forgive my father for abandoning me. I release him and cancel the debt."

5. Break the Vow in Jesus' Name
Use your authority in Christ to break the spiritual agreement. Declare: "I break the power of the inner vow that says I must be perfect to be loved. I break it in Jesus' name and declare I am loved because of who I am in Christ."

6. Replace the Vow with God's Truth
Ask the Lord, "What is Your truth about this area?" Write it down and declare it. For example: "God, I receive Your truth that I am safe in You. I don't have to protect myself. You are my defender."

Testimonies of Freedom

Sarah grew up with a verbally abusive father who constantly told her she was a failure. As a teenager, she vowed, "I'll prove I'm worth something." That vow led her into perfectionism, burnout, and anxiety. In an inner healing session, the Holy Spirit revealed the vow, and she wept as she renounced it.

When she heard Jesus say, "You are already worthy," a lifetime of striving broke off her soul.

Mark was sexually abused as a child. He vowed, "I'll never let anyone close." That vow protected him for years but also kept him lonely and guarded. During a healing retreat, God revealed the vow and the pain behind it. When Mark forgave, renounced the vow, and allowed Jesus into that wound, he experienced deep peace and began building real friendships for the first time.

Creating a Culture Free of Vows

Churches and families should be safe spaces to uncover and break inner vows. Pastors, counselors, and leaders must recognize the signs of these vows and walk people gently through the process of repentance and truth. We must create a culture where honesty, vulnerability, and Spirit-led healing are valued above performance and masks.

Inner vows lose their power in the light of God's presence. When we replace lies with truth, and fear with love, we experience the joy of emotional freedom and spiritual alignment. We stop living in the shadow of what hurt us, and we start living in the light of the One who heals us.

From Vows to Victory

Inner vows are silent chains, but the power of Jesus breaks every chain. Healing begins when we stop managing pain and start surrendering it. God doesn't want us living behind walls of self-protection. He wants us living as whole sons and daughters, fully known, fully loved, and fully free.

Let this be the moment where you say, "No more." No more making inner promises to guard your heart from pain. No more building fences where God wants to plant gardens. No more trusting yourself more than your Savior. Today, the vow breaks, and the truth of God rebuilds your life.

15

BREAKING INNER VOWS, UNGODLY BELIEFS, AND SOUL TIES

P ain does not simply pass through us — it imprints us. In moments of trauma, disappointment, betrayal, or fear, we often form inner conclusions that become silent agreements with the enemy. These are the inner vows, ungodly beliefs, and soul ties that keep us bound long after the external wound has seemingly healed. The work of inner healing requires not just identifying emotional pain, but breaking the spiritual contracts forged in it. In this chapter, we explore how to identify and sever these entanglements so that the truth of God can take root and freedom can flourish.

What Are Inner Vows?

An inner vow is a self-made promise formed in pain and enforced by fear. It sounds like: "I'll never trust anyone again." "I won't let anyone get close." "I'll always be the strong one." "I'll never be like my mother." These declarations are not idle words — they are soul-level agreements made to protect ourselves from being hurt again.

But what begins as a shield becomes a prison. Inner vows lock us into cycles of control, isolation, performance, and mistrust. We start shaping our lives not by truth or calling, but by what we're trying to avoid. These vows empower fear instead of faith and prevent the flow of love, intimacy, and even healing.

How Inner Vows Form

Inner vows are often formed in early childhood or adolescence — before we've even developed the maturity to understand pain, grief, or God's comfort. A child whose father leaves might vow, "I'll never need anyone." A teenager humiliated at school might vow, "I'll never let people see the real me again."

These vows are a form of inner control. In the moment of powerlessness, we try to reclaim authority through resolution — but instead of inviting God's help, we assume the role of protector ourselves. The problem is, these vows don't just guard us from pain — they guard us from love, vulnerability, and trust in God.

The Cost of Inner Vows

Inner vows shape our behavior and even our relationships with God and others. Someone with a vow to never show weakness may resist spiritual intimacy. A vow to always be in control will clash with the call to surrender. A vow to never rely on others may isolate us from community or marriage.

Over time, these soul commitments distort identity and sabotage destiny. They can feel like personality traits — but they are often trauma-based adaptations. Many people confuse their vow-based self with their true self in Christ. This is why the Holy Spirit gently brings these to the surface — not to shame us, but to invite freedom.

Ungodly Beliefs: The Lies We Live Under

Closely connected to inner vows are ungodly beliefs — false conclusions about God, ourselves, or others that take root in pain. These beliefs often sound like:

- "I am unlovable."
- "God doesn't really protect me."
- "People always leave."
- "If I fail, I am worthless."
- "My value is in my performance."

These beliefs create strongholds (2 Corinthians 10:4–5) that must be torn down by the truth. They become the lenses we see life through, filtering everything — even Scripture — through lies.

How Ungodly Beliefs Work

Ungodly beliefs become the framework of expectation in our hearts. If I believe people will always abandon me, I subconsciously sabotage healthy connection or overreact to small disappointments. If I believe I am not worthy of love, I either reject it or attach too quickly, looking for what only God can give.

These beliefs also block our ability to receive the truth of God's Word. We read *"nothing can separate us from His love"* (Romans 8:39) — but something in us whispers, "except my mess." Until these lies are confronted, truth will feel distant, impersonal, or ineffective.

Soul Ties: Unseen Attachments

Soul ties are emotional, spiritual, and sometimes sexual connections formed between two people. God designed soul ties for covenant relationships like marriage or deep spiritual family — but when formed in sin, trauma, manipulation, or codependency, they become unholy entanglements.

Soul ties can happen through:

- Sexual intimacy outside of covenant (1 Cor. 6:16)
- Intense trauma bonding
- Controlling or manipulative relationships
- Ungodly spiritual leadership or false prophetic relationships
- Co-dependent friendships or family dynamics

These ties create a pull in the spirit — a place of influence, control, or unfinished pain.

The Symptoms of Soul Ties

Unbroken soul ties often show up as:

- Replaying conversations or moments over and over
- Feeling unable to emotionally detach from someone
- Reacting to their name, voice, or presence with anxiety or confusion
- Experiencing torment, shame, or identity confusion connected to them
- Feeling like part of your identity is still wrapped up in them

These symptoms are not just emotional — they can be spiritual oppressions tied to lingering soul connections.

Breaking the Chains: The Power of Renunciation

Renunciation is the biblical act of canceling agreement with darkness. We break vows, reject lies, and sever ties — not just with words, but with faith and spiritual authority.

Here's a Spirit-led process:

1. Ask the Holy Spirit to Reveal.
Begin by praying: "Holy Spirit, show me any inner vow, ungodly belief, or soul tie that is blocking my freedom." Wait quietly. Memories, emotions, or phrases may rise to the surface.

2. Identify and Write Them Down.
Be specific. What was the vow? What lie did you believe? Who is the person you feel tied to?

3. Break the Inner Vow.
Say aloud, "In the name of Jesus, I break the inner vow that I will [state the vow]. I no longer place my trust in this vow. I release it and submit to the Lordship of Jesus."

4. Renounce the Ungodly Belief.
"I renounce the lie that [state the belief], and I receive the truth that [declare God's Word]."

5. Sever the Soul Tie.
"I break all unholy soul ties between me and [name], in the name of Jesus. I command every spiritual and emotional connection to be severed, and I take back every piece of my heart, identity, and purpose."

6. Forgive and Release.

Forgiveness is key. Say, "I forgive [name] for what happened. I release them into God's hands. They owe me nothing. I am free."

7. Invite the Holy Spirit to Fill the Space.
Say, "Holy Spirit, fill every place where lies once lived. Heal every place where pain had power. Restore my soul."

Declaring God's Truth Over Every Area

Freedom isn't just breaking what's wrong — it's embracing what's right. Once inner vows, lies, and ties are broken, we need to fill those places with God's truth, identity, and promises. Here are some declarations you can use:

- "I am not alone — I am loved, seen, and chosen."
- "I don't have to be in control — God is my refuge and strength."
- "I am no longer defined by my past — I am a new creation in Christ."
- "I receive God's perfect love that casts out fear."
- "My identity is not in performance but in being a beloved son/daughter."

Speak these aloud. Your words are powerful (Proverbs 18:21). You are establishing Kingdom reality over your inner world.

Healing Is a Journey

You may find that these vows, beliefs, or ties show up in layers. Don't be discouraged if you have to revisit an area more than once. Healing is not a one-time event — it's a lifestyle of walking in the Spirit, renewing the mind, and staying anchored in truth.

Each layer of freedom deepens your intimacy with Jesus and your ability to walk in love, truth, and purpose.

A Prayer to Break Inner Vows, Lies, and Soul Ties

Heavenly Father, I thank You that You desire truth in the inward parts. I come before You with an open heart. Reveal any vow I've made in pain, any lie I've believed in fear, and any tie that keeps me bound. In the name of Jesus, I break every inner vow I've made to protect myself apart from You. I place my trust in You alone. I renounce every ungodly belief and replace it with Your truth. I break every soul tie with people, places, or memories that are not from You. I take back every part of me and give You full access to heal me. Fill every place where darkness once lived. Let Your light and love flood my soul. I choose freedom, truth, and wholeness — in Jesus' name.
Amen.

A New Way of Living

Breaking inner vows, lies, and soul ties isn't just about deliverance — it's about restoration. You're not just casting off chains — you're reclaiming who you were always meant to be.

You are not the sum of your survival strategies. You are not the product of trauma or sin. You are a beloved child of God, called to live from a place of freedom, love, and truth.

Let every broken vow become a place of surrender. Let every shattered belief become a testimony of truth. Let every severed tie make space for holy connection. This is your time to walk free — from within.

16

ENCOUNTERING GOD IN THE PAIN

P ain often feels like a place of abandonment, yet it is here —right in the middle of our deepest wounds—that God waits to meet us. The Gospel is not a message of escape from pain; it is a promise of God's presence in the midst of it. When Jesus stepped into human flesh, He didn't avoid suffering—He entered it fully, embodying the ache of humanity. For many, pain becomes a silent prison, a fortress built to survive. But healing happens when the walls come down, when the presence of Jesus enters the memory, the feeling, the experience— and makes all things new.

This chapter explores how we create space to encounter God in the pain. We'll walk through Spirit-led methods of listening prayer, engaging memories, prophetic acts, and being present to the Holy Spirit. The goal is not just emotional release but divine exchange. Jesus doesn't simply observe our pain; He redeems it. When we meet Him in the wound, He speaks truth, brings safety, and restores what was lost.

1. Pain is a Place of Encounter

Throughout Scripture, God often chooses the painful places to reveal Himself. To Hagar, fleeing abuse and feeling unseen, He appeared as "El Roi"—the God who sees (Gen. 16:13). To Moses, disqualified and hiding, God spoke from the burning bush (Ex. 3:1–12). To Elijah, depressed and exhausted, He came not in the fire or earthquake, but in a whisper (1 Kings 19:11–13). The pattern is consistent: God meets His people in their brokenness. Pain is not a barrier to His presence; it's often the doorway.

Pain isolates and deceives. It tells us we are alone, unworthy, or irreparably broken. But the truth is, the very thing that makes you withdraw is the place where God wants to draw near. You may not feel Him, but He's there. And when invited, Jesus steps into the wound—not as a distant observer, but as a healer, shepherd, and friend.

2. Creating a Safe Space for Healing

Healing rarely happens in chaos. It begins with a space of intentional stillness—a room for your heart to breathe. In a busy, overstimulated world, one of the greatest gifts we can offer our souls is the quiet. Healing prayer begins with creating a sacred space: not just physical, but spiritual and emotional.

This means calming the nervous system, silencing outside voices, and preparing our hearts to listen. Some people play soft worship music, light a candle, or sit in a familiar chair. Others journal or take deep breaths to become aware of their own soul. But most importantly, we ask, "Jesus, will You meet me here?"

This space becomes holy ground. You're not just doing spiritual work—you're encountering the Living God. You are safe. You are seen. And you are not alone.

3. Listening Prayer — Inviting Jesus into the Wound

One of the most powerful forms of healing is listening prayer—a Spirit-led practice where we ask Jesus to show us what He sees and hears. Rather than analyzing pain or offering advice, we invite the Lord into the wound. He reveals what's hidden, speaks truth into the lies, and brings comfort that no words can.

Here's a simple structure for listening prayer:

1. Ask the Holy Spirit to lead — "Holy Spirit, will You guide this time? Protect me, and bring up only what You want to heal."
2. Ask Jesus to show the memory — "Jesus, is there a memory You want to heal right now?"
3. Observe what comes — Don't force anything. Often a childhood moment, a traumatic event, or a painful experience will come to mind. Sit with it. What do you feel?
4. Ask, 'Jesus, where are You in this memory?' — This is the most important part. Sometimes He appears visibly in the memory. Other times, you may sense His presence or hear Him speak.
5. Ask Him what He wants you to know — Jesus speaks truth into the lies you believed in that moment. He might say, "You were not alone," or "It wasn't your fault," or "You are still Mine."
6. Respond to what He shows you — This may include forgiving someone, renouncing a lie, or simply receiving comfort.

7. Invite Him to heal and restore — "Jesus, will You take the pain? Will You restore what was lost? What do You want to give me in exchange?"

This practice is not just about revisiting memories—it's about redeeming them. The Jesus who was always present brings you into truth, safety, and restoration.

4. Prophetic Acts and Symbolic Healing

Sometimes healing requires action, even if symbolic. Prophetic acts are simple physical expressions that mirror what's happening in the spirit. In Scripture, prophetic acts are often used to release God's power: Naaman washes in the Jordan seven times (2 Kings 5), Jesus puts mud on the blind man's eyes (John 9), Paul lays handkerchiefs on the sick (Acts 19).

Here are some examples of prophetic acts in healing prayer:

- Writing and burning a lie — Write the lie you believed ("I am unworthy," "God abandoned me") and burn it as a declaration that it no longer has power.
- Taking off a garment — Literally taking off a jacket to symbolize shedding shame, fear, or grief.
- Standing up — A powerful moment of rising from the pain, choosing freedom, and stepping into identity.
- Receiving a gift — Asking Jesus, "What do You want to give me in place of the pain?" and receiving by faith.

Prophetic acts help the body, soul, and spirit align with the truth. They declare, "This moment matters. Healing is real. I receive it fully."

5. Presence-Based Ministry — Not a Formula, but a Flow

Healing is not a technique—it's a relationship. Presence-based ministry means we follow the Holy Spirit, not a script. No two sessions look alike. Sometimes God brings up a specific memory. Other times, He brings emotion to the surface without explanation. We must stay attuned to what He's doing.

Here's what this requires:

- Sensitivity — Pay attention to shifts in emotion, posture, or thought. These are clues to what the Lord is touching.
- Surrender — Don't rush the process. Let the Holy Spirit lead.
- Silence — Sometimes the most powerful healing comes not in words, but in stillness.
- Scripture — God often brings a verse to mind that unlocks the moment. Declare it over the person.
- Spirit of Compassion — Healing is not about fixing someone. It's about loving them in their pain until Jesus touches them.

When we stay in the flow of the Spirit, even the most painful places can become altars of restoration.

6. Facing the Lie, Embracing the Truth

At the core of every wound is a lie—a false belief that was embedded in pain. "I'm not good enough." "I'm always alone." "I deserved it." The enemy sows these lies like seeds, and if left unchallenged, they grow into strongholds. The goal of healing is not just to feel better—it's to walk in truth.

Ask the Holy Spirit to reveal the core lie you believed in the painful moment. Then ask, "Jesus, what is the truth?" Often, the truth He speaks is simple yet profound: "You are Mine." "I never left." "You are clean." "You are loved."

The power of truth breaks the chains of the past. Jesus said, "You will know the truth, and the truth will make you free" (John 8:32). When truth enters the memory, it changes not only how we feel about it—but how we live moving forward.

7. Posture of the Heart — Becoming Like a Child

Healing is not about striving. It's about surrender. Jesus said, *"Unless you become like a little child, you cannot enter the Kingdom"* (Matt. 18:3). Inner healing requires a childlike posture: honest, vulnerable, trusting.

Let your heart become soft again. Let your tears flow. Let your defenses come down. The world told you to toughen up, but healing requires the opposite. The more you try to be strong, the harder it is to receive. You don't need to have the right words or emotions. You just need to come.

"Jesus, I don't know how to heal. But I give You my pain. Will You meet me here?"

And He will.

8. From Tears to Testimony — What Happens After

When Jesus touches a wound, there is almost always a shift.

Sometimes it's subtle—a sense of peace, a sigh, a deep breath. Sometimes it's dramatic—crying, shaking, laughter, release. But after every encounter, there is a decision to make: Will I walk in the truth I've received?

That may mean:

- Speaking differently about yourself
- Setting new boundaries
- Breaking a toxic agreement or relationship
- Living like the wound is no longer in control
- Replacing old behaviors with new habits of healing

Healing is not just about what happens in the session. It's about how you walk afterward. You are no longer the person who was wounded—you are someone Jesus has touched. Begin to speak, act, and live like it.

9. When Pain Comes Back

Healing is often layered. Sometimes after a powerful encounter, old feelings resurface. This doesn't mean the healing "didn't work." It means God is inviting you deeper.

Return to the place of encounter. Reaffirm the truth. Ask again, "Jesus, what do You want me to know?" The more you return to Him, the more your soul learns to live healed. Pain may knock at your door, but it doesn't own you anymore.

Remember: Healing is not an event. It's a journey of continual encounters with Jesus.

10. Jesus in the Middle

The true power of inner healing is this: not that we face our pain alone, but that we find Jesus in the middle of it. The cross is the ultimate declaration that God doesn't avoid pain—He enters it, transforms it, and resurrects it. Every time we invite Jesus into a wound, we are reenacting the Gospel. And every time we listen, trust, and receive His presence in our pain, we are being conformed into His image.

You are not just being healed—you are being transformed.

Let this become your prayer:

"Jesus, I give You access to my pain.
I open the locked doors.
I welcome You into the memories I've buried.
Speak Your truth. Heal what's broken.
Let Your light invade the shadows.
I believe You're not afraid of my pain—
You're drawn to it.
Because You love me.
And where You are, I am safe."

Let the encounter begin.

Reflection and Activation

- Set aside 30–60 minutes this week for a healing encounter. Find a quiet space, play worship, and invite the Holy Spirit to lead.
- Journal any memories, feelings, or lies that arise.
- Ask Jesus to show up in that space. Listen and write what He says.
- Perform a prophetic act to seal the moment.
- Declare aloud the truth you received from Jesus.

There is no wound so deep that Jesus cannot heal it. No pain so hidden that He cannot find it. And no place so dark that His light cannot shine into it. When we encounter God in the pain, we discover the beauty of redemption. We are not just survivors—we are sons and daughters being made whole.

17

HEALING THE INNER CHILD

Healing the inner child is a profound journey that involves revisiting and addressing the wounds of our early years. As believers, we are invited to bring these tender areas into the presence of Jesus, allowing His love and truth to bring restoration and wholeness.

Understanding the Inner Child

The concept of the "inner child" refers to the childlike aspects within an individual, encompassing both joyful and wounded parts. These facets influence our adult behaviors, emotions, and relationships. Unresolved childhood experiences can manifest as patterns of fear, insecurity, or dysfunctional relational dynamics. Recognizing and nurturing our inner child is essential for breaking free from these cycles.

In psychological terms, the inner child embodies the subconscious memories and feelings from our formative years. When these experiences are negative or traumatic, they can lead to maladaptive behaviors in adulthood. Engaging in inner child work involves acknowledging these past experiences and providing the care and support that was lacking during childhood.

Biblical Foundations for Inner Child Healing

Scripture underscores the significance of childlike faith and the value of children in the Kingdom of God. Jesus' interactions highlight His deep care for the young and the childlike:

"He called a little child to him, and placed the child among them. And he said: 'Truly I tell you, unless you change and become like little children, you will never enter the kingdom of heaven. Therefore, whoever takes the lowly position of this child is the greatest in the kingdom of heaven. And whoever welcomes one such child in my name welcomes me."
—Matthew 18:2-5 (NIV)

This passage emphasizes the purity, trust, and humility inherent in children—qualities that are often diminished by life's hardships. Restoring these attributes through healing allows us to experience the fullness of life in Christ.

Furthermore, the Bible speaks to God's desire to heal our brokenness:

"He heals the brokenhearted and binds up their wounds."
—Psalm 147:3 (NIV)

This assurance invites us to bring our wounded inner child to God for healing and restoration.

The Impact of Childhood Wounds

Unaddressed childhood wounds can profoundly affect our adult lives, influencing our self-perception, relationships, and spiritual walk. Common manifestations include:

- Fear of Abandonment: Stemming from experiences of neglect or loss, leading to clinginess or avoidance in relationships.
- Low Self-Esteem: Resulting from constant criticism or unmet emotional needs, causing feelings of inadequacy.
- Trust Issues: Developing from betrayals or inconsistent caregiving, making it difficult to rely on others or God.
- Perfectionism: Emerging from conditional love or high expectations, driving an incessant need to prove oneself.

These patterns can hinder our ability to fully embrace God's love and purpose for our lives.

Inviting Jesus into Childhood Memories

Healing begins by consciously inviting Jesus into our past experiences, allowing His presence to transform our pain. This process involves several steps:

1. Prayerful Reflection: Set aside quiet time to reflect on your childhood, asking the Holy Spirit to reveal memories that need healing.
2. Visualization: Imagine Jesus present in those moments, offering comfort, protection, and truth.
3. Dialogue with Jesus: Engage in a conversation with Christ about these experiences, expressing your feelings and listening for His response.

4. Receiving Truth: Allow Jesus to replace any lies or negative beliefs formed during those times with His truth and affirmations.

5. Forgiveness: With Jesus' help, choose to forgive those who caused harm, releasing the burden of resentment.

6. Embracing Your Inner Child: Acknowledge and accept this part of yourself, offering the love and care that was previously lacking.

This practice aligns with the biblical principle of renewing our minds:

"Do not conform to the pattern of this world, but be transformed by the renewing of your mind."
—Romans 12:2 (NIV)

By inviting Jesus into our memories, we allow Him to renew our minds and heal our hearts.

Practical Steps for Healing the Inner Child

Engaging in intentional practices can facilitate the healing process:

- Journaling: Write letters to your inner child, expressing love, validation, and understanding. Document any memories that surface and your feelings associated with them.
- Creative Expression: Utilize art, music, or dance to connect with and express the emotions of your inner child.
- Recreation: Engage in activities you enjoyed as a child, rekindling joy and playfulness.

- Affirmations: Speak positive, truth-based affirmations to yourself, countering negative beliefs rooted in childhood.
- Counseling: Seek guidance from a Christian counselor experienced in inner healing to navigate complex emotions and memories.

These steps, coupled with prayer and scripture meditation, create an environment conducive to healing.

Testimonies of Inner Child Healing

Hearing others' experiences can provide encouragement and insight:

- Sarah's Story: After years of struggling with feelings of unworthiness, Sarah invited Jesus into her memories of childhood neglect. Through prayer and counseling, she experienced a profound sense of love and acceptance, transforming her self-perception.
- David's Journey: Haunted by memories of early abuse, David sought inner healing through guided prayer sessions. By envisioning Jesus present during his traumatic experiences, he found peace and the ability to forgive his abuser.
- Maria's Experience: Maria engaged in creative journaling to connect with her inner child. Through this process, she uncovered suppressed emotions and, with the Holy

Integrating the Healed Inner Child into the Adult Self

The culmination of healing the inner child involves integrating this renewed aspect into our adult self, fostering a harmonious and whole identity. This integration is crucial for living out our God-given purpose with authenticity and freedom.

Steps Toward Integration:

1. Continuous Dialogue: Maintain an ongoing conversation with your inner child, acknowledging its presence and needs. This practice ensures that the healed child remains an active and valued part of your inner world.
2. Consistent Self-Care: Implement routines that nurture both the adult and child within you. Activities that balance responsibility with playfulness can reinforce this integration.
3. Set Healthy Boundaries: Establish boundaries that protect your well-being, ensuring that both your adult self and inner child feel safe and respected in relationships and environments.
4. Seek Supportive Communities: Engage with faith-based groups or support networks that understand and encourage the journey of inner child healing. Shared experiences can provide strength and accountability.
5. Celebrate Milestones: Recognize and celebrate progress in your healing journey. Affirmations of growth reinforce the integration process and encourage continued development.

Living as a Whole and Healed Individual

As the healed inner child becomes an integral part of your adult self, you'll likely experience:

- Enhanced Relationships: Interactions become more authentic and fulfilling, rooted in a secure sense of self.
- Increased Resilience: A unified self can better navigate life's challenges, drawing strength from a well-integrated identity.
- Deeper Spiritual Connection: With past wounds healed, your relationship with God can flourish, unencumbered by previous barriers.
- Authentic Joy: Rediscovering childlike wonder and joy enriches daily life, allowing you to fully embrace and enjoy the present.

Healing the inner child is a transformative journey that invites Jesus into the deepest recesses of our past, allowing His love and truth to mend wounds that have long influenced our lives. Through prayerful reflection, intentional practices, and the support of faith communities, we can integrate our healed inner child into our adult selves, leading to a life marked by authenticity, joy, and purpose. Embracing this process not only restores our own hearts but also equips us to extend compassion and understanding to others on their paths to wholeness.

18

THE POWER OF RENUNCIATION AND DELIVERANCE

I n the journey toward spiritual wholeness, understanding and engaging in the practices of renunciation and deliverance are pivotal. These processes empower believers to sever ties with past sins, demonic influences, and ungodly associations, thereby facilitating a life of freedom and alignment with God's purpose.

Understanding Renunciation and Deliverance

Renunciation involves the intentional act of rejecting and disowning past sinful behaviors, beliefs, or associations that are contrary to God's will. It is a conscious decision to turn away from darkness and embrace the light of Christ. Deliverance, on the other hand, refers to the process through which individuals are set free from demonic oppression or influence. While renunciation is the human act of rejecting sin, deliverance is the divine act of God removing the spiritual consequences and entities associated with that sin.

The Biblical Foundation for Deliverance

Scripture provides numerous accounts of deliverance, underscoring its significance in the believer's life. Jesus' ministry was marked by acts of deliverance, demonstrating His authority over demonic forces and His commitment to setting captives free.

In Mark 16:17 NIV, Jesus declares, *"And these signs will accompany those who believe: In my name they will drive out demons; they will speak in new tongues."* This passage highlights that deliverance is not only a part of Christ's ministry but also a sign that accompanies believers.

Identifying the Need for Deliverance

Recognizing the need for deliverance is the first step toward freedom. Certain patterns and behaviors may indicate demonic influence or oppression:

1. Persistent Sinful Habits: Struggling with recurring sins despite genuine efforts to overcome them may suggest a deeper spiritual bondage.
2. Unexplained Physical Ailments: Chronic illnesses without medical explanation can sometimes have spiritual roots.
3. Mental and Emotional Turmoil: Experiencing overwhelming fear, depression, or anxiety that doesn't respond to conventional treatments may indicate demonic oppression.
4. Spiritual Blockages: Difficulty in prayer, worship, or understanding Scripture can be a sign of spiritual interference.
5. Nightmares and Disturbances: Regularly experiencing disturbing dreams or sensing a malevolent presence during sleep.

Steps to Renounce Spiritual Ties and Walk in Freedom

Engaging in renunciation and deliverance involves a series of intentional steps:

1. Self-Examination and Confession
Begin with introspection, identifying areas of sin or ungodly associations in your life. Confess these to God, acknowledging their opposition to His will. As 1 John 1:9 assures, *"If we confess our sins, he is faithful and just and will forgive us our sins and purify us from all unrighteousness." NIV*

2. Renounce Ungodly Ties
Verbally renounce any past involvement with sinful behaviors, occult practices, or ungodly relationships. This act of renunciation is a declaration of your break from these ties. For instance, you might pray: "In the name of Jesus, I renounce any involvement with [specific sin or practice]. I reject its influence over my life and close any doors I have opened to the enemy through this involvement."

3. Forgive Offenses
Holding onto unforgiveness can create openings for demonic influence. Choose to forgive those who have wronged you, releasing them from any debt. Forgiveness is not condoning the offense but freeing yourself from its hold.

4. Break Soul Ties
Soul ties are deep emotional connections with others, which can be godly or ungodly. Ungodly soul ties, such as those formed through sexual immorality or manipu-

lative relationships, need to be severed. Pray: "Lord
Jesus, I break every ungodly soul tie formed between me
and [person's name]. I reclaim the part of myself that I
gave to them and return any part of them that I have
retained. Let this tie be completely severed in Jesus'
name."

5. Remove Occult Objects
Eliminate any items associated with past sinful practices
or occult involvement from your possession. This
includes books, jewelry, symbols, or artifacts that do not
honor God. Destroying these items is a physical act that
mirrors your spiritual commitment to purity.

6. Seek Deliverance Prayer
While personal prayer is powerful, seeking assistance
from mature believers or ministers experienced in deliverance can provide additional support. They can pray
with you, offering guidance and discernment
throughout the process.

7. Fill the Void with God's Presence
After deliverance, it's crucial to invite the Holy Spirit to
fill any areas vacated by demonic forces. Engage in
regular prayer, worship, and Scripture study to fortify
your spirit. Jesus warns in Matthew 12:43-45 about the
danger of an empty house, emphasizing the need to be
filled with God's presence.

Maintaining Deliverance and Walking in Freedom

Achieving deliverance is a significant milestone, but maintaining that freedom requires ongoing vigilance:

1. Cultivate a Life of Holiness
Commit to living according to God's standards, avoiding situations or behaviors that could reopen doors to the enemy.

2. Regularly Renew Your Mind
Immerse yourself in Scripture to continually align your thoughts with God's truth. Romans 12:2 encourages believers to be transformed by the renewing of their minds.

3. Stay Connected to a Faith Community
Engage with a local church or small group for accountability, encouragement, and support. Isolation can make one more susceptible to spiritual attacks.

4. Be Watchful and Prayerful
Remain alert to the enemy's schemes and maintain a robust prayer life. Ephesians 6:18 urges believers to *"pray in the Spirit on all occasions with all kinds of prayers and requests."*

5. Seek Ongoing Inner Healing
Deliverance and inner healing are not one-time events but parts of a lifelong journey. Even after spirits are cast out or ties are broken, the soul may still carry wounds that need healing. Keep allowing the Holy Spirit to uncover and address areas of brokenness, insecurity, trauma, or unresolved grief. This continual yielding leads to deeper freedom and maturity.

For some, deliverance brings immediate freedom; for others, it begins a layered process of freedom and healing over time. Just as trauma may come in layers, so does the healing.

Each layer God peels back reveals a new level of freedom He desires to bring. Stay surrendered.

Common Areas that Require Renunciation

Many people unknowingly open doors to demonic influence. Below are common areas where renunciation is needed:

1. Occult Practices
Things like horoscopes, tarot cards, ouija boards, crystals, witchcraft, yoga practices with spiritual roots, astrology, and new age rituals all open spiritual doors. These must be confessed and renounced completely.

2. Sexual Sin
Sex outside of God's covenant (including pornography, fornication, adultery, and homosexual activity) often creates ungodly soul ties and spiritual openings. Repent, renounce, and ask Jesus to cleanse and restore your purity.

3. Addictions
Addictions—whether to substances, food, social media, gambling, or other compulsions—often carry demonic strongholds that require both practical recovery steps and spiritual deliverance.

4. Curses and Inner Vows
Words spoken over you or by you in moments of pain can function like curses or inner vows: "I'll never trust anyone again," or "I always fail." Renounce these statements, break agreement with them, and declare God's truth in their place.

5. False Religions and Ancestral Worship
Involvement with false religions, idol worship, Freemasonry, Eastern mysticism, ancestral rituals, or generational covenants with false gods must be renounced. The blood of Jesus is stronger than every ancestral spirit.

6. Bitterness and Unforgiveness
Refusing to forgive opens the door to torment (Matthew 18:34-35). Forgiveness doesn't mean trust, but it does mean releasing the offender to God and choosing freedom over vengeance.

A Sample Prayer of Renunciation and Deliverance

You can use this framework to guide someone—or yourself—through a Spirit-led moment of renunciation:

"Father God, I come before You in the name of Jesus Christ, my Savior and Deliverer. I thank You that the blood of Jesus cleanses me from all sin. I confess and repent for any way I've opened doors to the enemy—knowingly or unknowingly—through sin, disobedience, trauma, or generational iniquity.
I renounce and break every agreement I've made with the enemy. I renounce (name specific sins, practices, or lies). I break every ungodly soul tie and spiritual tie connected to these things.
I forgive those who have hurt or abused me, and I release them to You, Lord. I ask You to break any generational curse, spirit, or stronghold that has passed down through my family line.
I declare that Jesus Christ is my Lord. I belong to Him and Him alone. I close every door to the enemy, and I command every unclean spirit to leave me now in the name of Jesus. Holy Spirit, fill every place in me that has been cleansed. Restore my soul, renew my mind,

and fill me with Your peace and truth. Thank You for my freedom. I receive it by faith. In Jesus' name, amen."

The Role of Fasting in Deliverance

Fasting can be a powerful weapon in the deliverance process. Jesus said in Matthew 17:21 (NKJV), "However, this kind does not go out except by prayer and fasting." Fasting humbles the soul and weakens the flesh, creating a greater sensitivity to the Spirit. It's not about earning freedom, but about increasing spiritual clarity and authority.

Whether it's a one-day fast or a three-day water fast, ask the Holy Spirit to lead you. Use the time to worship, read Scripture, and ask God to expose hidden strongholds. Fasting often brings breakthrough when other efforts have plateaued.

Deliverance Is Not a Substitute for Discipleship

Many people seek deliverance hoping for a "quick fix," but freedom must be followed by formation. Jesus didn't just cast demons out—He called people to follow Him. Discipleship solidifies your deliverance. Without it, the ground cleared of demonic influence may become vulnerable again.

Inner healing helps you understand why the stronghold was there to begin with. Deliverance casts out what's tormenting you; discipleship teaches you how to never let it back in.

So after deliverance:

- Get rooted in a Bible-teaching, Spirit-led church.
- Build accountability and community.
- Learn to hear God's voice daily.

- Feed on the Word.
- Walk in obedience, not just emotion.

Deliverance in the Ministry of Jesus

A true deliverance ministry should always point people to Jesus—not to fear, formulas, or fascination with demons. Jesus had authority and peace when casting out demons. He didn't yell, sensationalize, or entertain evil spirits. He simply commanded them to leave.

Deliverance should never be weird, controlling, or emotionally abusive. It should be marked by the fruit of the Spirit— love, joy, peace, patience, kindness, goodness, faithfulness, gentleness, and self-control. If the Holy Spirit is truly present in a deliverance session, then His nature will be, too.

Jesus operated with both truth and love. He delivered Mary Magdalene (Mark 16:9), the boy with seizures (Mark 9), the man in the synagogue (Luke 4), and the Gadarene demoniac (Mark 5). Each of them was restored in dignity, peace, and identity.

If Jesus needed deliverance to be part of His ministry, then so do we.

Deliverance Must Be Paired with Healing

Deliverance is powerful—but it is not the whole picture. It must be married to healing. In many cases, a demon is hiding in a wound, using trauma or pain as legal access to stay. If you cast the spirit out but never heal the wound, it may return later or another spirit may take advantage of the broken place.

This is why inner healing and deliverance must go hand in

hand. Where healing happens, the enemy loses territory. When the wound is sealed by truth and presence, the spirit has no more foothold.

If someone has dissociative parts, protectors, or fractured identities, these must be gently integrated and healed before— or alongside—deliverance. Otherwise, the inner system can collapse or retraumatize. Always minister with compassion, not just confrontation.

Deliverance is Ongoing for Many

Some people experience a dramatic, one-time deliverance. Others walk through deliverance over a series of months. Don't compare your journey to others.

God knows what you're ready for. Sometimes He delivers layer by layer so your soul has time to heal, grow, and integrate. What matters most is not how quickly you get free—but how deeply and permanently you stay free.

If a spirit tries to return (through dreams, temptations, or attacks), stand firm. Don't panic. Resist the devil and he will flee (James 4:7). Plead the blood of Jesus, declare truth, worship, and remind yourself: "Whom the Son sets free is free indeed" (John 8:36).

Ending Strong: Your Freedom Has Purpose

Freedom is not just about relief from torment—it's about stepping into Kingdom purpose. When you get delivered, you're not just free from something—you're free for something. You're free to love boldly, to worship fully, to serve without shame, to walk in authority, and to lead others into freedom.

Your testimony of deliverance carries power. What God did for you, He wants to do through you. As you walk in the power of the Holy Spirit, you become a vessel of healing for others.

Deliverance is not just a ministry—it's a demonstration of the Gospel. Jesus came to destroy the works of the devil (1 John 3:8), and when you engage in renunciation and deliverance, you are continuing His mission.

You are not crazy. You are not too far gone. You are not disqualified. If you are in Christ, you are a new creation. The old has gone. The new has come.

Stand in your freedom. Guard it. Nourish it. And lead others into it.

You have been delivered, not just to survive—but to thrive.

19

GRIEVING WELL
ALLOWING PAIN TO PROCESS

Grief is an inevitable part of the human experience. It touches everyone, transcending age, culture, and faith. For believers, grief not only challenges our emotional resilience but also our spiritual convictions. Understanding how to navigate grief through the lens of faith can lead to profound healing and a deeper relationship with God.

Understanding Grief from a Biblical Perspective

The Bible does not shy away from the reality of grief. Throughout Scripture, we encounter individuals who faced profound sorrow and loss. Job, for instance, experienced the devastation of losing his children, wealth, and health. His lamentations are raw and unfiltered, reflecting the depths of his anguish. Yet, amidst his suffering, Job's dialogue with God reveals a journey toward understanding and eventual restoration.

In the New Testament, Jesus Himself embodies the human experience of grief. When Lazarus died, Jesus wept alongside

Mary and Martha, demonstrating that sorrow is a natural response to loss (John 11:35). His empathy underscores the importance of acknowledging and expressing grief rather than suppressing it.

The Necessity of Mourning

Mourning is the outward expression of internal grief. It allows individuals to process their emotions, confront the reality of their loss, and begin the journey toward healing. Ecclesiastes 3:4 reminds us that there is "a time to weep and a time to laugh, a time to mourn and a time to dance." Recognizing and honoring the season of mourning is crucial for emotional and spiritual well-being.

Suppressing grief can lead to unresolved emotional issues, manifesting in physical ailments, depression, or strained relationships. Conversely, embracing the mourning process facilitates healing. As Kris Vallotton notes, "Mourning is necessary; it's the process that leads to wholeness." —Kris Vallotton

Common Misconceptions About Grief

Misunderstandings about grief can hinder the healing process. Some common misconceptions include:

- Time Heals All Wounds: While time can provide perspective, it does not automatically heal grief. Active engagement in the grieving process is essential.
- Faith Eliminates Grief: Some believe that strong faith should preclude feelings of sorrow. However, biblical figures like David and Jesus Himself

expressed grief, indicating that faith and mourning can coexist.

- Moving On Means Forgetting: Healing does not necessitate forgetting the loved one or the loss. Instead, it involves finding a way to remember and honor them while continuing to live.

Steps to Process Grief Healthily

1. Acknowledge the Pain: Denial can prolong suffering. Recognize the loss and allow yourself to feel the associated emotions.
2. Seek Support: Surround yourself with a community of faith, friends, or support groups. Sharing your grief can alleviate the burden and provide comfort.
3. Engage in Prayer and Scripture: Turning to God's Word can offer solace and guidance. Verses like Psalm 34:18, *"The Lord is close to the brokenhearted,"* remind us of His presence during our darkest times.
4. Allow Yourself to Mourn: Give yourself permission to cry, reminisce, and express your feelings. Mourning is a personal journey; there's no "right" way to do it.
5. Avoid Isolation: While solitude can be healing, prolonged isolation can lead to deeper despair. Balance alone time with social interactions.
6. Consider Professional Counseling: Seeking help from a Christian counselor can provide tools to navigate complex emotions and offer a safe space to process grief.

The Role of Forgiveness in Grieving

In some instances, grief is intertwined with feelings of anger or resentment, especially if the loss involves perceived injustices or unresolved conflicts. Forgiveness becomes a pivotal step in the healing journey. As Vallotton emphasizes, "Forgiveness is the first step out of pain, but not the last" —Kris Vallotton[1]. By forgiving others, ourselves, or even circumstances, we release the hold that bitterness can have on our hearts.

Embracing the Hope of Resurrection

For Christians, the hope of resurrection offers profound comfort in times of grief. The promise of eternal life and reunion with loved ones provides a perspective that transcends temporal sorrow. As Jesus assured Martha, "*I am the resurrection and the life. The one who believes in me will live, even though they die*" (John 11:25 NIV). This hope does not negate the pain of loss but offers assurance of God's ultimate plan for redemption and restoration.

Practical Ways to Support Others in Grief

As members of the body of Christ, we are called to "mourn with those who mourn" (Romans 12:15 NIV). Supporting others through their grief involves:

- Being Present: Sometimes, the ministry of presence speaks louder than words. Simply being there can provide immense comfort.
- Listening Without Judgment: Allow the grieving person to share their feelings without offering unsolicited advice or platitudes.
- Offering Practical Help: Assist with daily tasks, provide meals, or help with errands. These acts of

service can alleviate some of the burdens during a difficult time.
- Encouraging Professional Support: If appropriate, suggest seeking counseling or joining a support group.

The Transformative Power of Grief

While grief is undeniably painful, it can also be transformative. Walking through the valley of sorrow can lead to:

- Increased Empathy: Personal experiences of loss can deepen our compassion for others who are suffering.
- Renewed Faith: Wrestling with grief can lead to a more profound and resilient faith as we experience God's comfort and provision.
- Clarified Priorities: Loss often prompts reflection on what truly matters, leading to a reevaluation of life's priorities.

Grieving well is not about adhering to a set timeline or prescribed steps but about allowing oneself to authentically experience and process loss. By integrating faith into the grieving process, believers can find solace in God's promises, support within the Christian community, and hope in the resurrection. Remember, mourning is a journey, and with God's grace, it can lead to healing and renewed purpose.

Honoring the Grief Journey Without Idolizing Pain

One of the most delicate tensions to navigate in grief is allowing space for pain without making pain the centerpiece of your identity. There is a danger in becoming so attached to sorrow that it begins to define who you are. This can happen subtly when grief becomes the filter through which we see ourselves and the world around us.

Grief must be honored—but never enthroned. It's not your identity, it's a season. Pain has a voice, but it must not be given the microphone indefinitely. Many believers struggle because they confuse honoring grief with empowering it. You can honor grief by acknowledging your loss, lamenting in God's presence, and processing it in healthy ways. But empowering grief means giving it authority over your life, letting it steal your joy, dictate your choices, and silence your destiny.

Jesus meets us in our sorrow to walk us through it—not to let us build a house in the valley of the shadow. He anoints our heads with oil in the presence of our enemies (Psalm 23:5), even when grief surrounds us. His presence is not to make us comfortable in loss but to empower us to walk forward in hope.

Walking With God Through the Stages of Grief

The grieving process is often described through five primary stages: denial, anger, bargaining, depression, and acceptance. While these stages are not linear and don't apply to every individual in the same order, they provide a framework for understanding the journey[2].

As a believer, it's important to bring God into each of these emotional stages:

- Denial: When you're in shock or disbelief, ask God to gently help you face the truth with grace. Invite the Holy Spirit to soften the blow and provide the courage to face what has happened.

- Anger: Express your anger to God honestly. He is not afraid of your emotions. David cried out in frustration, and yet God called him a man after His heart. Bring your rage to the altar—it's safer there than suppressed in your soul.
- Bargaining: In this stage, many try to make deals with God or replay "what if" scenarios. Instead of bargaining, learn to trust God's sovereignty. Surrender the outcome you hoped for and invite Him into your questions.
- Depression: When sadness becomes overwhelming, ask God to sit with you in the darkness. He is Emmanuel—God with us. Even if you feel numb, speak the truth of His nearness over your soul.
- Acceptance: This is not about forgetting or approving of the loss, but about integrating it into your story and moving forward with grace. Acceptance means choosing life, even in the face of death.

God's grace is present in every stage. He doesn't rush you through grief, but He does promise to walk with you in it and eventually lead you out of it.

Scriptural Lament as a Tool for Healing

Lament is not complaining—it's a biblical, Spirit-led response to pain and loss. The book of Lamentations, many Psalms, and even Jesus' cry on the cross (*"My God, my God, why have you forsaken me?"*) are examples of sacred lament.
Lament includes:

1. Addressing God — Come to Him honestly.
2. Describing the pain — Be real about what hurts.

3. Asking for help — Petition for justice, healing, or mercy.
4. Choosing trust — Declare God's faithfulness, even when you don't feel it.

Psalm 13 is a powerful example. David begins with deep sorrow and confusion, but ends with trust: *"But I trust in your unfailing love; my heart rejoices in your salvation"* (Psalm 13:5 NIV).

Teaching your soul to lament helps you process pain with God rather than apart from Him. It keeps you from spiritual suppression or emotional isolation and invites intimacy into suffering.

Letting Go Without Letting Go of Love

A core fear in grief is that by letting go, we're betraying the memory of a person or minimizing the loss. But letting go of the pain is not the same as letting go of love. In fact, healing allows love to be remembered with gratitude instead of only with agony.

You are allowed to let go of:

- Bitterness
- Regret
- Guilt
- Questions that have no answers
- The illusion of control

You are never asked to let go of:

- The impact that person made
- The good memories
- The legacy of love

- The hope of seeing them again in eternity

Letting go is about opening your hands so God can place something new in them—not about erasing the past, but about releasing it into His hands.

When the Grieving Process Feels Stuck

Some believers find themselves stuck in prolonged grief that seems to linger beyond healthy mourning. This is often referred to as "complicated grief." It can be a result of:

- Sudden or traumatic loss
- Unresolved guilt or anger
- Codependent relationships with the deceased
- Unprocessed childhood trauma being re-triggered

If you feel stuck in grief:

1. Ask the Holy Spirit for revelation: What part of your heart is still bound?
2. Invite Jesus into the pain: Often, a core memory needs to be healed or revisited.
3. Consider inner healing prayer: Many find breakthrough through sessions where the Holy Spirit is invited to lead the process.
4. Renounce lies: Lies such as "I'll never be happy again" or "I should have done more" must be replaced with God's truth.
5. Declare freedom: Speak life over your soul. Declare that your heart will heal, that joy will return, and that you will live again.

Stuck grief is not shameful—it's a cry for deeper healing. God sees it and wants to walk with you through it.

Rebuilding Your Life After Loss

Grief dismantles the world as we knew it. The life we expected, the routines we shared, and even the dreams we held are suddenly changed. Part of grieving well is choosing to rebuild with God's help.

Rebuilding involves:

- Rediscovering identity: Who are you now? Let Jesus remind you that your identity is not in your loss but in His love.
- Reestablishing rhythms: Healthy routines— spiritual, physical, and relational—create new structure for your soul to grow in.
- Rediscovering joy: It will feel risky at first. Laughter may feel wrong. But joy is not betrayal—it is proof that death did not win.
- Reimagining purpose: Many who've walked through grief find a renewed sense of purpose—advocating for others, serving in compassion, or writing their testimony. Let the pain give birth to purpose.

Grief does not mean your life is over. In fact, it can be the fertile ground where a new version of life emerges—one that's deeper, more authentic, and grounded in eternity.

The Comforter is Still With You

John 14:16–18 promises that the Holy Spirit is our Comforter. The Greek word "Parakletos" means one who comes alongside to help. In grief, we don't just need answers—

we need presence. And the Spirit of God is faithful to be exactly that.

He comforts:

- Through Scripture
- Through silence
- Through worship
- Through nature
- Through others
- Through divine whispers in the night

Ask the Holy Spirit to comfort you—not just in concept, but in tangible, personal ways. He will. He is close to the broken-hearted. You are not alone in the night.

Activating Grief Into Compassion

The final stage of healing is often when the grief you carried becomes fuel for healing others. You don't have to rush this step, but it's powerful when it comes.

Grief gives you:

- Empathy others can't fake
- Language for the hurting
- Strength to sit in sorrow without fixing
- Authority to declare healing because you've walked through pain

You become a wounded healer—someone who doesn't just quote truth, but embodies it. Someone who doesn't rush people through pain, but walks them through it with love. You are proof that healing is possible.

Activation: Grieving With God

Reflective Questions:

1. What losses have I experienced that I've never fully grieved?
2. Am I angry at God, myself, or others—and have I brought that honestly to the Lord?
3. Have I let grief become my identity, or am I allowing God to walk me through it?
4. What is one truth from Scripture I can hold onto in this season?

Prayer of Surrender:

Father, I bring You my sorrow, my questions, my pain. I thank You that You do not despise my grief, but You draw near to it. Teach me how to mourn with hope. Help me to let go without losing love. I invite the Holy Spirit to be my Comforter in this valley, and I trust that You will lead me through it. I declare that this pain will not define me—Your love will. Let my heart be made whole again, in Jesus' name. Amen.

In Summary:

Grieving well is not about forgetting or rushing—it's about inviting God into the sorrow and letting Him walk with you through the shadows. Pain does not disqualify you from purpose; rather, when surrendered, it becomes a wellspring of compassion and power.

In the Kingdom, we grieve, but not as those without hope. We cry, but we do not collapse. We remember the cross and the empty tomb—and we know that even in our grief, resurrection is coming. And until that day, we walk hand-in-hand with the God who weeps with us... and heals us from within.

20

REBUILDING IDENTITY AND PURPOSE
RECEIVING A NEW NAME AND IDENTITY FROM JESUS

Throughout Scripture, God bestows new names upon individuals to signify a transformation in their identity and purpose. Abram became Abraham, Sarai became Sarah, Jacob became Israel, and Simon was named Peter. Each renaming marked a pivotal shift aligned with God's divine plan for their lives. This pattern underscores a profound spiritual principle: encountering God redefines who we are.

In the New Testament, Saul's transformation into Paul exemplifies this concept. Once a persecutor of Christians, Saul's encounter with Jesus on the road to Damascus led to his new identity as Paul, a devoted apostle of Christ. This change was not merely nominal but reflected a deep, internal renewal and a reoriented mission. Similarly, when we come to Christ, we are invited into a new identity. 2 Corinthians 5:17 declares, *"Therefore, if anyone is in Christ, the new creation has come: The old has gone, the new is here!"** This passage emphasizes that our past no

---

* NIV

longer defines us; instead, our identity is rooted in the redemptive work of Jesus.

Embracing this new identity involves shedding the labels and limitations imposed by past experiences, failures, or societal expectations. It requires us to see ourselves through God's perspective, recognizing that we are His beloved children, chosen and set apart for His purposes. This transformation is both instantaneous in our spiritual standing and progressive in our daily walk, as we continually align our self-perception with God's truth.

Walking in Restored Confidence, Calling, and Joy

Understanding and accepting our new identity in Christ naturally leads to a restored sense of confidence. This confidence is not rooted in our abilities but in the assurance of God's presence and empowerment. Philippians 1:6 NIV reassures us: *"Being confident of this, that he who began a good work in you will carry it on to completion until the day of Christ Jesus."* Recognizing that God is actively working in and through us instills a profound sense of security and boldness.

Our calling emerges from this renewed identity and confidence. Ephesians 2:10 NIV reveals, *"For we are God's handiwork, created in Christ Jesus to do good works, which God prepared in advance for us to do."* Each of us has a unique purpose designed by God, and as we walk in our new identity, we become attuned to His specific plans for our lives. This calling may manifest in various forms—vocational pursuits, ministry opportunities, or daily interactions—but all are avenues through which we can glorify God and serve others.

Joy is a natural byproduct of living in alignment with our

God-given identity and purpose. Nehemiah 8:10 NKJV reminds us, *"The joy of the Lord is your strength."* This joy transcends circumstances, rooted in the unchanging nature of God's love and the fulfillment found in walking according to His design. It empowers us to navigate challenges with resilience and to radiate hope to those around us.

Prophetic Acts and Declarations of Destiny

Throughout the Bible, prophetic acts serve as tangible expressions of faith, symbolizing and enacting God's promises. For instance, the prophet Elisha instructed King Joash to strike the ground with arrows to symbolize victory over his enemies (2 Kings 13:14-19). Such actions demonstrate a physical alignment with spiritual truths, reinforcing belief and anticipation of God's intervention.

In our journey of rebuilding identity and purpose, engaging in prophetic acts can be a powerful means of solidifying our commitment and faith. This might involve writing down and publicly declaring God's promises over our lives, participating in symbolic actions that represent leaving behind old identities, or embracing new roles that reflect our renewed purpose. These acts serve as milestones, marking our transformation and dedication to God's calling.

Declarations of destiny involve verbally affirming our identity and purpose in alignment with Scripture. Proverbs 18:21 NKJV states, *"Death and life are in the power of the tongue"* By speaking God's truth over our lives, we reinforce our faith and counteract negative narratives that may have previously shaped our self-perception. Regularly declaring statements such as "I am a child of God," "I am called and equipped for good works," and "The joy of the Lord is my strength" can transform our mindset and embolden us to live out our divine purpose.

Rebuilding our identity and purpose is a transformative journey that begins with embracing the new name and identity bestowed upon us by Jesus. This foundational shift cultivates restored confidence, clarifies our calling, and fills our lives with enduring joy. Engaging in prophetic acts and declarations serves to solidify these truths, enabling us to walk boldly in the destiny God has prepared for us. As we align our lives with His vision, we become living testimonies of His redemptive power, reflecting His glory to the world around us.

21

HEALING IS A LIFESTYLE

Healing is not a moment; it is a way of life. While encounters with God can bring powerful transformation in a single moment, sustaining wholeness requires a lifestyle anchored in intimacy with the Father, alignment with truth, and intentionality in how we live, think, feel, and relate. Healing isn't merely about resolving past trauma; it's about learning how to steward the wholeness God has given us, day by day, decision by decision.

The journey of inner healing brings us to a crossroads where we must choose to live healed. Many believers experience powerful freedom only to find themselves slipping back into old patterns, triggers, or broken relationships. Why? Because healing must become integrated into how we live—not just what we experience in prayer sessions or altar calls.

This chapter will walk through what it means to adopt a healing lifestyle: one of discipline, intimacy with Jesus, emotional self-awareness, spiritual authority, and healthy boundaries. It will call you to maturity—no longer living by default but by design.

1. Choosing Wholeness Daily

Healing begins with decision. Just like salvation starts with a "yes" to Jesus, healing starts with a "yes" to being whole. But after the initial breakthrough, we face choices each day: Will I respond from my new healed self or from old wounds? Will I partner with truth or fall back into old lies?

To choose wholeness is to refuse to let old patterns, fears, or labels define us. It is a continual renewing of the mind (Romans 12:2) and a yielding to the Spirit's leading rather than the soul's dysfunction.

This doesn't mean pretending you're fine when you're not. It means when your pain surfaces, instead of suppressing it or reacting from it, you pause and invite Jesus into it. You make space for processing rather than projecting. You choose the voice of the Spirit over the voice of trauma.

2. Disciplining Your Soul and Renewing Your Mind

A lifestyle of healing requires training the soul. David said in Psalm 131:2 NKJV, *"Surely I have calmed and quieted my soul."* That's an act of discipline. Emotions are valid but not always accurate. Feelings are indicators, not dictators.

To live healed is to take responsibility for your inner world. Paul wrote in 2 Corinthians 10:5 NIV that we are to *"take every thought captive to make it obedient to Christ."* That's active work. It means recognizing toxic or trauma-based thoughts and submitting them to truth.

This is why reading Scripture, journaling, soaking in worship, and meditating on God's promises aren't just spiritual disciplines—they are healing practices. They reprogram our soul to align with Heaven rather than hellish mindsets rooted in fear, rejection, shame, or pride.

3. Staying in Intimacy With the Father

Wholeness flows from the Father's heart. Jesus said, *"Abide in me"* (John 15:4). When we stay close to Him, we receive ongoing nourishment, identity, and correction. Many people lose their healing not because God took it back, but because they drifted from the Vine.

Intimacy is the wellspring of sustained healing. In His presence, we're reminded of who we are and whose we are. In worship, the lies lose their grip. In prayer, our inner man is strengthened. In quietness, we hear His truth louder than our pain.

A healing lifestyle doesn't just include moments with God —it revolves around Him. You make space for Him every day, not just when things are falling apart.

4. Recognizing Triggers as Opportunities

Triggers don't mean you've failed. They mean there's something inside you that still needs tending. A healed life doesn't ignore triggers; it investigates them with the Holy Spirit.

Ask: Why did that comment bother me so deeply? Why did I withdraw, get defensive, or overreact? What part of me feels unsafe, unseen, or unloved?

When triggers happen, it's a gift. They reveal hidden wounds or unresolved agreements. Instead of shame or condemnation, let your triggers lead you to deeper healing. Let them be invitations for Jesus to go deeper.

This practice makes you spiritually and emotionally mature. You no longer let your life be run by your pain—you learn to respond, not react.

5. Walking in Community With Healthy Accountability

We are healed in relationship. Yes, some parts of the journey require solitude with Jesus, but many wounds happened in community—and they must be healed in community.

Living healed means inviting safe people into your journey. Not everyone, but a few trusted individuals who know the real you, who can lovingly correct you, and who walk with you through your ups and downs.

This is where spiritual family matters. You need fathers, mothers, mentors, and peers who aren't impressed by your gifts but care about your soul. Living healed is being accountable, teachable, and vulnerable.

James 5:16 NIV says, *"Confess your sins to one another and pray for each other so that you may be healed."* Healing multiplies in safe relationships. Isolation stunts growth. Transparency fosters transformation.

6. Creating Boundaries to Protect Peace

Healing doesn't just involve dealing with internal pain; it

also involves making external choices that protect your peace. That's where boundaries come in.

A healed lifestyle includes knowing when to say no, when to walk away, when to pause a conversation, and when to create space. You are not called to be everyone's healer or rescuer. You are responsible to people, not for people.

Jesus had boundaries. He withdrew often. He said "no" to certain requests. He confronted dysfunction. He refused to be manipulated by crowds or individuals. Why? Because His identity and assignment came from the Father, not from people's opinions or expectations.

Boundaries aren't walls to shut people out; they're gates to protect what's holy within. Your peace is sacred. Guard it with wisdom and grace.

7. Keeping a Short List — Walking in Forgiveness

Unforgiveness is a slow leak in your healing journey. It may not seem like a big deal at first, but over time, it depletes your emotional and spiritual life.

Living healed means keeping a short list. Don't let offense, bitterness, or disappointment take root. Deal with it quickly. Forgive freely. Ask for forgiveness humbly.

This doesn't mean excusing abuse or enabling toxicity. It means releasing people from the debt they owe you and trusting God to deal with them. It means prioritizing your freedom over your right to be right.

Forgiveness is maintenance for the soul. It keeps your heart light and your spirit free. Make it a habit, not just an event.

8. Practicing Gratitude and Celebrating Progress

Healing can feel like slow progress, especially when you're in the middle of it. That's why gratitude is essential. It helps you recognize how far you've come, not just how far you have to go.

Celebrate small wins. Did you handle that conversation better than you would've last year? Praise God. Did you notice a trigger but chose peace instead of reaction? Celebrate. Did you go a week without spiraling into shame? Rejoice.

Gratitude shifts your perspective from lack to abundance. It reminds your soul that God is at work even when it's not dramatic. Thanksgiving is a healing lifestyle. Psalm 100:4 says, "Enter His gates with thanksgiving..." Gratitude brings you into God's presence daily.

9. Continuing the Work of Inner Healing

Living healed means staying open to ongoing healing. Wholeness isn't a one-time destination; it's a continual journey. As we mature, the Holy Spirit reveals deeper layers of pain, pride, insecurity, or unmet needs.

This is not regression—it's growth. God peels back the layers as we are ready. Be willing to go back to Him as needed. Ask the hard questions. Sit in His presence when He stirs something up. Don't run from discomfort—embrace it as an invitation to go deeper.

Even years after your initial healing, you may find new

areas needing Jesus' touch. That's not a sign you're broken again. It's a sign you're becoming whole.

10. Living With Eternity in View

Ultimately, healing isn't just about us—it's about becoming who God created us to be so that we can reflect His glory on the earth. When you live healed, you live for something greater than comfort—you live for Kingdom impact.

Your healing becomes a testimony, your wholeness a weapon, your peace a signpost pointing others to Jesus. The world needs believers who are whole—not perfect, but healed. People who can carry the weight of love, truth, and spiritual authority.

Live as one who has been raised from the dead. Walk with boldness. Let your healed life point to the Healer.

Final Activation

Here are some practical daily practices to help you live healed:

- Daily check-in: Ask your soul, "How are we doing today?" Listen. Then ask, "Holy Spirit, what do I need to know or receive?"
- Journaling truth: Write down lies you're tempted to believe and replace them with Scripture-based truth.
- Worship atmospheres: Fill your home and car with worship. Let praise be the soundtrack of your healing.

- Pause moments: When you feel triggered, pause. Breathe. Invite Jesus into the moment. Ask Him what's really going on.
- Soul care rhythms: Prioritize rest, hobbies, beauty, and community. Your soul needs joy, not just responsibility.

Becoming Whole People in a Broken World

A healing lifestyle is a prophetic witness in a chaotic world. You become a safe place for others. You become a living example of God's power to redeem, restore, and renew.

You're not perfect, but you're present. You're not unshakable, but you're anchored. You're not immune to pain, but you don't live from it anymore.

Healing is no longer something you chase—it's how you live. You walk with Jesus into every area of your heart, soul, mind, and body. You choose peace, humility, and honor. You guard your heart, not out of fear, but because it is the wellspring of life (Proverbs 4:23).

You are living healed. And the world is watching.

22

BECOMING A HEALER
HELPING OTHERS WALK IN WHOLENESS

Embarking on the journey of inner healing is transformative, not only for personal restoration but also for equipping individuals to guide others toward wholeness. As we experience the profound healing power of Jesus in our own lives, we are called to extend that healing to those around us. This chapter delves into the principles and practices essential for leading others through inner healing, ministering safely and effectively, and fostering a culture of healing within our churches and ministries.

The Call to Minister Healing

Scripture is replete with instances where Jesus commissions His followers to continue His healing ministry. In Matthew 10:8 NIV, Jesus instructs His disciples: "*Heal the sick, raise the dead, cleanse those who have leprosy, drive out demons. Freely you have received; freely give.*" This mandate underscores the responsibility and privilege we have as believers to be conduits of God's healing power.

Understanding the Role of a Healing Minister

A healing minister serves as a facilitator, creating an environment where individuals can encounter Jesus, the true Healer. This role requires deep empathy, active listening, and a reliance on the Holy Spirit's guidance. It's imperative to recognize that the minister is not the source of healing but a vessel through whom God's power flows.

Essential Qualities of an Effective Healing Minister

1. Personal Wholeness: Before guiding others, it's crucial to address one's own wounds and seek personal healing. Unresolved issues can hinder the minister's effectiveness and potentially harm those they aim to help. As highlighted in a discussion on healing after church hurt, leaders must confront their own unhealed wounds, as personal healing is essential to effectively guide others through their spiritual journeys.

2. Deep Empathy and Compassion: A genuine love for others, mirroring Christ's compassion, is foundational. This involves entering into another's pain without judgment and offering a safe space for vulnerability.

3. Active Listening Skills: True healing begins when individuals feel heard. Active listening involves fully engaging with the speaker, reflecting back what is heard, and withholding immediate advice or solutions.

4. Spiritual Discernment: Sensitivity to the Holy Spirit's leading is vital. This discernment helps in identifying root issues, understanding the spiritual dynamics at play, and knowing how to pray effectively.

5. Commitment to Confidentiality: Trust is the bedrock of healing relationships. Upholding confidentiality ensures that individuals feel safe to share deeply without fear of exposure.

Steps to Leading Others Through Inner Healing

1. Establish a Safe Environment: Begin by creating a setting where the individual feels secure and valued. This includes choosing a private, comfortable space and setting clear boundaries.

2. Build Rapport and Trust: Take time to connect on a personal level. Share appropriate aspects of your own journey to demonstrate empathy and understanding.

3. Invite the Holy Spirit's Presence: Acknowledge that true healing comes from God. Begin with prayer, inviting the Holy Spirit to lead the session and reveal what needs to be addressed.

4. Explore Presenting Issues: Allow the individual to share their story at their own pace. Use open-ended questions to facilitate deeper exploration of feelings and experiences.

5. Identify Root Causes: With the Holy Spirit's guidance, discern underlying issues or past traumas that contribute to current struggles. This may involve revisiting painful memories to bring them into the light.

6. Facilitate Forgiveness and Renunciation: Guide the individual in forgiving those who have caused harm and renouncing any lies or vows formed in response to

pain. This step is crucial for breaking spiritual strongholds.

7. Replace Lies with God's Truth: Help the individual to hear from Jesus, receiving His truth to counteract the lies they've believed. This can be facilitated through prayer and listening for God's voice.

8. Pray for Healing and Deliverance: Offer prayers for emotional, spiritual, and physical healing. Address any demonic influences if discerned, ensuring that deliverance is conducted with the individual's consent and in alignment with scriptural principles.

9. Empower and Equip: Provide the individual with tools and resources to maintain their healing, such as scripture readings, prayer strategies, and recommendations for ongoing support.

10.Follow-Up and Support: Healing is often a journey rather than a one-time event. Schedule follow-up meetings to offer continued support and address any new issues that arise.

Ministering Safely and Effectively

Safety in healing ministry is paramount, both for the minister and the recipient. Implementing the following safeguards ensures ethical and effective ministry:

1. Operate Within a Team: Whenever possible, minister alongside others. This provides accountability, additional discernment, and support.

2. Set Clear Boundaries: Define the scope of your ministry and adhere to it. Avoid dual relationships (e.g., being both a counselor and a friend) that can blur lines and lead to complications.

3. Recognize Your Limits: Acknowledge when an individual's needs exceed your expertise. Be prepared to refer them to professional counselors or medical professionals when necessary.

4. Maintain Continuous Education: Stay informed about best practices in inner healing, psychological insights, and theological understandings. Attend workshops, read relevant literature, and seek mentorship.

5. Prioritize Self-Care: Regularly assess your own emotional and spiritual health. Engage in practices that replenish you, such as personal retreats, counseling, and spiritual direction.

Creating a Culture of Healing in Your Church or Ministry

Fostering an environment where healing is a normative part of church life requires intentionality:

1. Teach on Healing: Regularly incorporate teachings on God's desire and power to heal into sermons and Bible studies. This raises awareness and builds faith within the congregation.
2. Offer Training Programs: Equip members with the skills to minister healing by providing

In the journey toward personal wholeness, a profound transformation occurs when one extends the grace of healing to others. This chapter delves into the sacred calling of becoming a healer, offering guidance on leading others through inner healing, ministering safely and effectively, and fostering a culture of healing within your church or ministry.

Understanding the Call to Heal

Healing is central to Jesus' ministry. He not only restored physical health but also mended broken hearts and spirits. As His followers, we are invited to participate in this restorative work. The Apostle Paul emphasizes this in his letter to the Galatians:

"Carry each other's burdens, and in this way you will fulfill the law of Christ." (Galatians 6:2 NIV)

Embracing the role of a healer means stepping into a partnership with the Holy Spirit to facilitate healing in others.

Preparing Yourself for Healing Ministry

Before ministering to others, it's essential to undergo personal preparation:

1. Deepen Your Relationship with God: Regular prayer and immersion in Scripture cultivate sensitivity to the Holy Spirit's guidance.
2. Seek Personal Healing: Address your own wounds to minister from a place of wholeness and authenticity.
3. Educate Yourself: Understand the principles of inner healing through study and training. Resources like "A Guide for Listening and Inner-Healing Prayer" by Rusty Rustenbach provide valuable insights.

Leading Others Through Inner Healing

Ministering healing involves several key components:

1. Create a Safe Environment: Establish trust by ensuring confidentiality and demonstrating empathy.
2. Listen Actively: Pay close attention to the individual's story, allowing the Holy Spirit to reveal underlying issues. As Christian Healing Ministries advises, "Always follow the guidance of the Holy Spirit, asking Him to reveal any blocks to healing that need to be prayed through."
3. Identify Root Causes: Help individuals uncover the origins of their pain, which may include past traumas, unforgiveness, or false beliefs.
4. Facilitate Forgiveness and Renunciation: Guide them in forgiving those who have caused harm and renouncing lies they've believed.
5. Invite Jesus into the Wounds: Encourage them to envision Jesus present in their painful memories, bringing truth and healing.
6. Pray for Deliverance and Restoration: Seek the Holy Spirit's intervention to break strongholds and restore the individual to wholeness.

Ministering Safely and Effectively

To ensure a responsible healing ministry:

1. Maintain Ethical Boundaries: Avoid dual relationships and respect personal boundaries.
2. Collaborate with Professionals: Recognize when to

refer individuals to licensed counselors or medical professionals.

3. Continual Learning: Stay informed about best practices in pastoral care and counseling.

4. Supervision and Accountability: Engage in regular supervision with experienced mentors to reflect on your practice and receive feedback.

Creating a Culture of Healing in Your Church or Ministry

Fostering an environment where healing is a shared value involves:

1. Teach on Healing: Regularly incorporate teachings on God's desire to heal into sermons and Bible studies. As highlighted by Seedbed, "Educate the community of faith concerning Divine Healing."

2. Provide Training: Equip members with the skills to minister healing through workshops and seminars.

3. Offer Healing Prayer Opportunities: Create spaces during services or special gatherings for individuals to receive prayer.

4. Share Testimonies: Encourage individuals to share their healing stories to build faith and expectation.

5. Cultivate a Supportive Community: Promote small groups where members can journey together toward healing.

Becoming a healer is a sacred journey that requires personal preparation, reliance on the Holy Spirit, and a commitment to ethical practice. By leading others through inner healing and fostering a culture of restoration, you participate in the transformative work of God's Kingdom, bringing wholeness to individuals and communities alike.

CONCLUSION
FROM BROKENNESS TO BEAUTY

There is a divine thread woven through every story of healing—an invisible yet powerful testimony of a God who specializes in transformation. The journey of inner healing is not merely about recovery; it is about resurrection. From the ashes of pain, God brings beauty. From the ruins of trauma, He builds testimony. From brokenness, He creates wholeness. This is the promise of the Kingdom: that no wound is too deep, no past too shattered, and no life too far gone for the healing touch of Jesus.

In the pages of this book, we've traced a path—through hidden pain, soul fragmentation, lies rooted in trauma, and the many masks worn to survive. We've sat in the presence of Jesus, allowed Him to speak truth into wounds, and partnered with the Holy Spirit to remove barriers that block intimacy and destiny. Now, as this written journey closes, we step into the greater call that wholeness leads to: becoming a vessel of healing for others, and walking in the fullness of a restored life that reflects the glory of God.

The God Who Heals Everything

From the very beginning, healing has been at the heart of God's mission. When humanity fell, He did not discard us. Instead, He pursued, covered, restored, and promised redemption. Throughout Scripture, God reveals Himself as Jehovah Rapha—the Lord who heals. Not just physically, but emotionally, spiritually, relationally, and generationally.

Healing is not an optional side project in the Kingdom; it is central to the Gospel. Jesus did not only come to forgive sin, but to heal the brokenhearted (Luke 4:18), to set captives free, and to bind up wounds that cannot be seen by the naked eye. Wholeness is His intention for us—body, soul, and spirit.

As you reflect on your own healing journey, remember that God never wastes pain. Every scar, every tear, every step of transformation becomes part of the masterpiece He is crafting in you. You are not the same person who began this journey. You are being shaped into someone who carries healing within, someone who reflects the heart of the Father.

You Are Becoming a Healer

One of the greatest truths of the Kingdom is this: God heals us so that we can help heal others. Inner healing is not an end; it is an equipping. As you have received comfort, you are now able to comfort others with the same comfort you've received from God (2 Corinthians 1:3–5). The healing that once felt so personal now becomes a ministry, a lifestyle, a divine assignment.

You may not feel ready. That's normal. Many who have walked through trauma or deep emotional wounding wrestle with the thought of being used by God to help others. But remember—your authority doesn't come from perfection. It comes from your healing. Your wholeness becomes your warfare. Your story becomes someone else's roadmap. Your scars become signs that the power of God is real.

You are not just a survivor. You are a son. A daughter. A carrier of glory. A representative of the Kingdom. A restorer of paths for others to walk in.

Healing doesn't require a pulpit, a microphone, or a counseling degree. It requires availability, compassion, and a willingness to stay close to Jesus. As you minister to others—whether in a conversation, a prayer, or a simple act of love—you are releasing the Kingdom. You are embodying what it means to be healed from within.

Living from a Place of Wholeness

Healing is not just something we receive. It's something we carry. Wholeness becomes a way of living—how we think, speak, respond, lead, and love. It impacts how we build relationships, make decisions, steward our families, lead our ministries, and influence our communities.

To live from a place of wholeness means:

- You no longer react from pain, but respond from peace.
- You no longer carry shame, but walk in sonship.
- You no longer strive for identity, but live from it.
- You no longer suppress emotion, but process it with truth and safety.
- You no longer live guarded, but discerning and surrendered.

Wholeness empowers you to thrive—not just function. It means you can love deeply, dream boldly, risk freely, and forgive fully. It means you can walk through storms without drowning in despair. It means you can lead others with integrity because you've let God lead you through your own valley.

And yes, the journey continues. Healing is not a one-time event; it is a continual invitation. There will be new layers, new memories, new revelations. But now you walk equipped. You've developed language, tools, and confidence. You know how to invite Jesus into the pain. You know how to listen. You know how to partner with the Holy Spirit. You've been trained in truth, and now you carry it.

The Culture of Healing

Imagine a church where healing isn't just a ministry, but a culture. A place where confession is met with compassion. Where weakness is not punished, but pastored. Where emotions are not dismissed, but discerned. Where altars are not just for salvation, but restoration.

You are part of building that culture. Whether in your family, small group, ministry, or organization, your healing shapes the atmosphere around you. As you live in wholeness, you give others permission to do the same. You model safety, vulnerability, and grace. You point others to the One who heals the soul.

This culture does not form through programs—it forms through people. Through you. Through your story. Through your willingness to stay soft in a hard world. Through your decision to forgive, to bless, to speak life, and to walk humbly with God.

When churches become places of healing, people stop hiding. Marriages are restored. Leaders become whole. The next generation grows up with emotional literacy and spiritual authority. Demonic strongholds break. Revival flows not just from stages, but from hearts made whole.

The Eternal Perspective

Healing is beautiful not only because of what it does in this life—but because of what it points to in the next. Every moment of healing, every victory over trauma, every lie dismantled, and every tear wiped by Jesus is a foretaste of eternity.

Revelation 21:4 NIV gives us a glimpse: "He will wipe every tear from their eyes. There will be no more death or mourning or crying or pain..." This is the fullness of restoration. This is where the story is heading. And yet, through Jesus, we are allowed to taste it now. The Kingdom is both now and not yet. Heaven invades earth every time a soul is made whole.

You are a living signpost of that Kingdom. Your healing declares that Jesus is alive. Your story says to the world: "There is hope. There is freedom. There is a God who sees and saves."

And even in the unresolved places, the waiting rooms of our stories, we trust that He is not finished. Healing is not the absence of hardship—it is the presence of Jesus in the middle of it. The same Jesus who wept at Lazarus' tomb, who bled for your wounds, who rose to give you victory, is with you now. Healing always leads us to Him.

Final Charge: Rise and Walk

To the one who has walked this journey through the pages of this book: well done. You have faced what many run from. You have invited Jesus into places that were locked for years. You have chosen truth over numbness, courage over comfort, and vulnerability over control. And you are rising.

Now it's time to walk. Walk in the identity you've reclaimed. Walk in the peace you've received. Walk in the authority you carry. Walk in the love that has redefined you. And as you walk, look around—because others are waiting. Waiting for someone to tell them healing is possible. Waiting for someone to show them the way. Waiting for someone like you.

You don't have to be perfect to be powerful. You don't have to have all the answers to lead others into truth. You simply have to be healed from within, and willing to bring others along.

Let your voice be heard. Let your story be told. Let your heart remain soft. Let your home be a refuge. Let your hands bring healing. Let your life be a living epistle of grace and glory.

You are not just healed.
You are a healer.
You are not just restored.
You are a restorer.
You are not just whole.
You are a house where the Healer dwells.

From brokenness to beauty.
From trauma to testimony.
From surviving to shining.

From the inside out.

Welcome to the journey.
Welcome to wholeness.
Welcome to the Kingdom.

"The Spirit of the Sovereign Lord is upon me, because the Lord has
anointed me to proclaim good news to the poor.
He has sent me to bind up the brokenhearted,
to proclaim freedom for the captives
and release from darkness for the prisoners...
to bestow on them a crown of beauty instead of ashes,
the oil of joy instead of mourning,
and a garment of praise instead of a spirit of despair.
They will be called oaks of righteousness,
a planting of the Lord
for the display of his splendor." (Isaiah 61:1–3 NIV)

Amen.

NOTES

19. Grieving Well

1. Kris Vallotton, "How to Process Pain When Time Isn't Healing Your Wounds," *Kris Vallotton*, April 5, 2019.
2. Jim Daly, "Walking Through the Healing Process," *Daly Focus* (Focus on the Family), April 23, 2021.

ABOUT THE AUTHOR

Tom Cornell is the Senior Leader of SOZO Church in Washington state, founder of Walk in the Light International and SOZO N

etwork. Tom is married to his beautiful wife Katy and lives in the Puget Sound area with her and their three kids. He has been in ministry pastoring and teaching the body of Christ since 2008.

He has a passion to see the body of Christ moving from people with an orphan mindset to that of sonship; equipping the body to do the work of Jesus resulting in seeing the Kingdom of God manifested here on earth.

www.ingramcontent.com/pod-product-compliance
Lightning Source LLC
LaVergne TN
LVHW052024080426
835513LV00018B/2152